THE
TWO DOORS
INTO
ETERNITY

DR. FRANK W. PARSONS

PUBLISHED BY FIDELI PUBLISHING, INC.

Two Doors Into Eternity

Copyright © 2025, Frank Parsons

Unless otherwise noted, all Scripture is quoted from the
New American Standard Bible, 2020
by the Lockman Foundation, La Habra, Calif.

ISBN: 978-1-962402-18-7

Published by

Fideli Publishing, Inc.
119 W. Morgan St.
Martinsville, IN 46151

www.FideliPublishing.com

PRINTED IN THE UNITED STATES OF AMERICA

*This book is dedicated to all who are faithfully warning
people of the pending wrath of God*

Preface

I doubt many people think about *eternity* until we come near to the end of our life. Then, maybe some of us might start to come to grips with reality of eternity. Unfortunately, many people are so consumed with *secularism, materialism, things of this world,* and *fiery passions* of the carnal nature. It is not surprising then that we give little thought about eternity. For many of us as humans, eternity is like a child's mind: *out of sight, out of mind.*

Well, friend I am here to tell you that you had better think about eternity. Eternity is the real. Eternity is only a breath away, and death is no respecter of persons whether young or old. So, eternity is reality that is awaiting every human being that ever lived. Death is the real commencement.

Life now on this earth is only a *flicker, a moment in time.* But then, the light goes out in this world but **The Two Doors into Eternity** open to the real commencement that begins. Depending on which door you chose (*yes, you chose*), that door is sealed behind you. There is no turning back or reprieve. Your fate is sealed by your own doing forever and ever.

The Epistle of James compares our life as nothing more than *a vapor* or just a "single breath" that immediately disappears. Then, my friend, our life instantly vanishes from this world. The Bible says,

> Come now, you who say, "Today or tomorrow we will go to such and such a city, spend a year there, buy and sell, and make a profit"; [14] whereas you do not know what *will happen* tomorrow. For what *is* your life? It is even a vapor [e.g., *a single breath of air*] that appears for a little time and then vanishes away. [15] Instead you *ought* to say, "If the Lord wills, we shall live and do this or that." [16] But now you boast in your arrogance. All such boasting is evil. [17] Therefore, to him who knows to do good and does not do *it*, to him it is sin.   (James 4:13-17 NKJ)

Life is brief, and life seems extremely brief when it is compared to the door into eternity. Unfortunately, the forces of darkness, the devil and the other evil angels, are also working to blind the minds of people.[2 Cor. 4:3, 4] Satan is blinding people of the reality of eternity. (As I said above, we do not think about the reality of eternity because "It is out of sight, out of mind.")

Yes, eternity is coming. Eternity awaits every person whether they believe it or do not believe it. The reality of eternity continues forever after death. Here is the dreadful and terrifying reality that the door into Hell awaits everyone that is without Jesus Christ as their Lord and Savior! I mean everyone without Jesus Christ as Savior will surely spend eternity in Hell.

The fool and mocker have the same mindset. The fool has no sense; he is oblivious to everything around him. He is void of any reasoning. He is totally ignorant of facing eternity. The mocker is wise in his own eyes. He just blatantly denies eternity exists, and at death, this ends all. So, the mocker is much worse than a fool. As Solomon said,

> I have seen a man who seemed to himself to be wise; but a fool had more hope than he [*does*].　　　　　　　　　　　(Prov. 26:12 LXE)

In addition, the mocker disregards the Word of God as nothing more than some writing of the natural man. He fails to realize that the Bible is indeed the Word of Life. God in His infinite mercy is *beckoning* to him to take the *water of life* and live forever in the glories of Heaven with Christ Lord. As the risen Lord Jesus said,

> And he said unto me, It is done. I am Alpha and Omega, the beginning and the end. I will give unto him that is athirst of the fountain of the water of life freely.　　　　　　　　　　　(Rev. 21:6 KJV)

Sadly, the mocker is worse than a fool because he is wise in his own eyes. He cannot listen to correction; neither can he hear the truth of God's Word. Oh friend, how is it that a person can be so brilliant and intelligent, but he is so thoughtless and even worse than a fool?

I am appealing to everyone reading this book to please be very certain that you have genuinely repented and committed your life to Jesus Christ. I am appealing to everyone not only that they have genuinely committed their life to Christ, but they are now walking in obedience of faith in the Lord Jesus and His Word. I am also appealing to you that you are studying the Word of God in a faithful church, and you are indeed serving the Lord with all your heart and mind. As the apostle says so clearly,

And let the peace of Christ **rule** in your hearts, to which indeed you were called in one body. And **be thankful**. [16] Let the **word** of Christ **dwell in you richly**, teaching and admonishing one another in all wisdom, singing psalms and hymns and spiritual songs, with thankfulness in your hearts to God. [17] And whatever you do, in word or deed, **do everything in the name of the Lord Jesus, giving thanks** to God the Father through him. [23] Whatever you do, **work heartily, as for the Lord** and not for men, (Col. 3:15-17, 23 ESV)

Furthermore, I am hopeful that being in a faithful church and studying God's Word, you have a sincere and burning desire to share with your loved-ones and friends the Gospel, the Good News that Jesus Christ came into this world to save sinners.

[15]It is a trustworthy saying and deserving full acceptance: that **Christ Jesus came into the world to save sinners**, among whom I am foremost [*of sinners*]. [16] Yet for this reason I was shown mercy, so that in me as the foremost [*of sinners*], Christ Jesus might demonstrate all His patience as an example **for [*all*] those who are going to believe upon Him for eternal life**. [17] Now to the King of the ages, immortal, invisible, the only God, *be* honor and glory forever and ever. Amen.

(1 Tim. 1:15-17 LSB)

Yes, my friend, it is true; Jesus came to save any sinner, even the worst of sinners. As the apostle said before King Agrippa,

And Agrippa said to Paul, "In a short time would you persuade me to be a Christian?"

And Paul said, "Whether short or long, I would to God that not only you [*trust in Christ*] but also all who hear me this day might become such as I am [*trust in Christ*] — except for these chains." (Acts 26:28, 29 ESV)

But a Christian is not someone who espouses to just intellectually believe the Bible and attends church. A Christian is a person who has been **born from above by the Spirit** of the living God. He/she has genuinely committed to **complete trust in Christ** Jesus as their **personal Lord and Redeemer**. As result of their genuine faith in Christ, every genuine Christian is now a **citizen of Heaven** forever and ever. Hallelujah and amen!

My friend, I am making every effort to declare that there are only two doors into eternity. There is one door that opens into eternity which is Heaven. This door into Heaven which is God's abode, and Heaven is available to everyone that wants to enter through Jesus Christ. Yes, Heaven is indeed available to everyone who desires to be with the Lord.

Unfortunately, fools, mockers, and unbelievers do not care, and they are foolishly not interested due to their disbelief. Such people do not care either because they are a fools without reason and because they do not believe God's Word, the Bible. Therefore, they shall perish forever in Hell because of their unbelief.

However, please listen, God has given us His Word in order that **we can know** for certain that we can have eternal life and have it today. Listen carefully, here is how a person can receive eternal life and they can transfer their citizenship in this world and be a citizen of Heaven today. Yes, today you will have citizenship in Heaven. Heaven is real and your home is available in Heaven today. The Good News is Heaven is free to everyone that will genuinely repent and receive Jesus as their Lord and Savior.

The Bible declares clearly,

> I have written these things to you who believe in the name of the Son of God so that **you may know that you have eternal life**.
>
> (1 John 5:13 NET)

In addition, I want to share some things about Heaven. Regrettably, there are seemingly endless *deceivers, fraudulent liars, counterfeit preachers and teachers*, and *naive* leading millions astray. These are people who are deceiving people. There are people claiming that they have gone to Heaven and returned to tell us about Heaven. I am telling you right now: **do not believe them; they are deceiving liars**.

There are only two men of God that had actually gone to Heaven and returned. These two men are the only ones that went to Heaven and actually returned and possess the God given ability to tell us about Heaven. These were the apostles Paul and John. Yes, each ascended to Heaven, and they each returned to earth. However, the Lord God did not allow either man to reveal anything about Heaven. Paul and John were not permitted to reveal anything they saw or heard in the heavenly realm. Furthermore, there are no other mortal men who entered the heavenly realm and return and able to tell us. (Yet, there are endless charlatans and liars who claim to have gone to Heaven; but friend, I do not believe them and neither should you.)

Allow me to share with you exactly what the apostle Paul said concerning himself when he returned from Heaven.

> I know a man [Paul is referring to himself] in Christ who fourteen years ago (whether in the body or out of the body I do not know, God knows) was

caught up to the third heaven.[a] [3]And I know that this man (whether in the body or apart from the body I do not know, God knows) [4]was caught up into paradise[a] and **heard things too sacred to be put into words, things that a person is not permitted to speak.** (2 Cor. 12:2-4 NET)

[a]Note: "Third Heaven" is like the abode of God. The first heaven would likely be the sky immediately above. The second heaven is the stars above.

"Paradise," an expression for Heaven, a place of the blessed.

Neither apostle was permitted to reveal what they heard or things they saw in Heaven. In addition, consider this, Paul wrote at least thirteen epistles, Dr. Luke, one of his chief companions, wrote the Gospel of Luke and Acts (nearly the same amount of material as Paul). This alone is two/thirds the NT. If we add the epistle of Hebrews (which is possibility a Pauline epistle), then, Paul is the overwhelmingly primary theologian and teacher of the NT.

Therefore, if Paul was not permitted to tell us about Heaven, all those from years gone by and today that claimed to have enter Heaven and returned from Heaven to tell us about it are either: *crackpots, delusional, deceived by Satan's illusions, or liars*. Such *crackpots* are claiming revelational knowledge or divine insight. (Hence, these false teachers are claiming inspiration, which is a lie.) The Bible is clear that God's revelation and divine insight is sealed! So, anyone claiming revelation from God is mistaken; but unfortunately, others are either deceived or they are boldface liars of the worst sort.

Therefore, I am warning you my friend, do not believe such nonsense from such people claiming to have gone to Heaven and returned to tell us about it. Put your trust in what God has said in His Word, the Bible. Friend, the deception is only going get worse. Many people shall be led astray, and it is only going to get worse as our Lord said.

> [22]"If those days had not been cut short, no one would survive, but for the sake of the elect those days will be shortened. [23]At that time if anyone says to you, 'Look, here is the Messiah!' or, 'There he is!' do not believe it. [24]For false messiahs and false prophets will appear and **perform great signs** and **wonders to deceive**, if possible, even the elect."
>
> (Matt. 24:22-24 NIV)

Deception by Satan and evil angels will be very great as we approach the end times.

[8]And then the lawless [*the antichrist*] one will be revealed, whom the Lord will consume with the breath of His mouth and destroy with the brightness of His coming. [9]The coming of the *lawless* [*the antichrist*] *one* is according to the **working of Satan, with all power, signs**, and **lying wonders**, [10]and with all unrighteous deception **among those who perish**, [*perishing*] because they **did not receive the love of the truth, that they might be saved.** [11]And **for this reason God will send them strong delusion, that they should BELIEVE THE LIE**, [12]that they all may **be condemned who did not believe the truth** but had pleasure in unrighteousness.

(2 Thess. 2:8-12 NKJ)

It may be that ***demon oppression***[1] (not demon possession) is so very active among genuine believers by planting false doctrine in the mind or deceiving illusion among high profile Christian leaders.[2 Cor. 11:3; Matt. 16:22, 23] Listen, the devil works among those that are genuine believers, but he is working among false prophets as well.[1 Kings 22:16-23] Demons are likely oppressing many and may be deceiving some of the most internationally men and women of the Gospel across the entire world. (And if demon oppression is occurring among some of high-profile ministers, there is no way to know for certain.) Therefore, you better give heed because many, many people are likely to be deceived and believe **THE LIE**!

Some will classify me as an *alarmist*. "So be it!" An alarmist is defined as, "someone who is considered to be exaggerating a danger and so causing needless worry or panic." Also, meaning "the problem is a fabrication by alarmists."[2] I am not writing to cause worry or panic, but I am here to warn you that the wrath of God is coming upon all unregenerate without measure.

Friend, if there is such demon oppression occurring today, there is no way to know with any certainty. However, there are many Christian leaders that seemingly have departed from the central core of the fundamentals of the faith. This is possible due demon oppression. However, I do not think a genuine Christian can be demon possessed: "- greater is He who is in you than he who is in the world."[1 John 4:4b]

There are such large departures from the faith today that demon oppression is one possible explanation. So, demon oppression is a likely possibility, but whether there is a large scale of demon oppression, only the Lord knows. One thing is very certain, many Christian leaders have *departed from the faith*. Moreover, *many saints are void of spiritual discernment*. So, I think it is wise to be alert and watch out for demon activity which our Lord warns us.

Footnote:

1. "Demon oppression:" this is where Satan or one of the demons may insert thought into the mind, but evil spirits cannot control the mind. The Bible gives us this exhortation,

> For though we live as human beings, we do not wage war according to human standards, [4] for the weapons of our warfare are not human weapons, but are made powerful by God for tearing down strongholds. We tear down arguments [5] and every arrogant obstacle that is raised up against the knowledge of God, and **we take every thought captive to make it obey Christ**. (2 Cor. 10:3-5 NET)

The person being oppressed is likely unaware of the implant or inserted thought. They may even imagine the thought is from God, [2 Cor. 11:13-15]. This is why the Bible warns us "*to test the spirits*."[1 John 4:1] Regrettably, many saints have very poor spiritual discernment nowadays, and this makes some saints an easy prey by the evil spirits.

2. An "alarmist," from Google, a definition by Oxford Languages.

Table of Contents

Part Three
Absence of God's Presence but only condemnation

Part Four
Choose Eternal Life

Introduction

The style and study of this volume by the author is similar to his other writings. There is no change in the formatting. For example, there is the memory verse(s) in the beginning of the chapter. (This is to encourage to memorize Scripture, which is a necessity in a Christ-centered walk.) There is also a brief introduction and a short conclusion at the end. Also, at the top of each page, there will be the *chapter title* on one side of page and *on the opposite page there is the chapter subtitle*. I am encouraged that this particular format is helpful for the reader and working through *"Two Doors into Eternity"* more effectively. As in previous writings by the author, there are occasional footnotes, which you will read, that have been placed at the end of each chapter. In addition, at the end of the book, you find a list of acronyms, an index, and other books, tracts, and songs by Dr. Parsons.

As many may know, Scripture quotations are from various translations. The various translations have been used for variety of purposes but especially for clarity in some text. When Scripture is quoted in a separate paragraph, the texts will be indented and in smaller fonts. When Scripture quotations are within the paragraph, the font size remains the same size within the paragraph. The Scripture quotations will be from the New American Standard, 2020, and from the 1995 *updated* edition unless noted in the text. Some of the other major Scripture quotations are from the Geneva Bible (GNV) 1599; King James Version (KJV) 1611; American Standard Version (ASV) 1901; New Revised Standard (NRS) 1989; New English Translation (NET) 2005; the New International Version (NIV) 2011; English Standard Version (ESV) 2011; the Berean Study Bible (BSB) 2016; the Majority Standard Bible (which uses the BYZ text, 2022). There are other quotes from the Aramaic Bible in Plain English (ABPE) 2010; and the Common English Bible (CEB) 2011. There are quotes from the Literal Standard Version 2020.

If a Hebrew (HEB) or a Greek (GK) word is given, the word is spelled out phonetically in English (ENG). Small and large brackets ([], []) are used to indicate a word or phrase is added to clarify the Scripture text, but the insertion is not part of the original translation. The GK OT is quoted in the ENG from Septuagint [LXX] by Brenton (1851). When the author uses personal paraphrases, the word(s) are placed in *italics and indented*.

There are occasional footnotes at the end of the chapter as noted above. The footnotes are placed at end of each chapter for quick reference but to avoid disruption of the reading. The footnotes are for those who are inclined to probe more into the subject. Similarly, for the clarity of a word, there are inserted *like footnote fashion* in the Scripture texts quoted and place at the bottom of the text. For example, instead of a footnote at end of the chapter, the author has also added notes in brackets within the main text of Scripture but in a reference format. In addition, occasional footnotes, these are marked by footnote letter, e.g., [a], but the brackets "[]" are sometimes omitted. Please keep in mind that annotations are placed in the text similar to footnotes but remain in the text for immediate clarity. For instance,

> —if it [*the judgment of God*] begins with us [*the saved*], what will the outcome be for those who do not obey the gospel of God? And, "If it is hard [GK *molos, difficulty* or *scarcely*] for the righteous [a]to be saved, what will become of the ungodly and the sinner?" (1 Peter 4:17, 18 NIV)

[a]Note: this is the imputed righteousness we received through genuine faith in Christ Jesus through the Holy Spirit.[Rom. 8:30 1 Cor. 1:30; 6:11] The Bible is clear *there is no righteous, no not one.*[Ecc. 7:20; Rom. 3:10]

Here another example,

> [21]"Not everyone who says to Me, 'Lord, Lord,' shall enter the kingdom of heaven, but he who does the will of My Father in heaven. [22]"Many will say to Me in that day, 'Lord, Lord, have we not prophesied[b] in Your name, cast out demons in Your name, and done many wonders in Your name?' [23]"And then I will declare to them, '**I NEVER KNEW YOU**; depart from Me, you who practice lawlessness!' (Matt. 7:21-23 NKJ)

[b]Note: the person is relying on his "good works" to enter Heaven. However, eternal life is a "free gift" through genuine saving faith in Christ and being *born from above by the* sanctifying work of the Holy Spirit.

The insertions are to keep the flow going for reader but provide an immediate clarity without disrupting the flow and reading.

For those who are a little more meticulous, the GK NT with various readings and difference by variance in translations are usualized. This includes consulting various HEB and GK lexicons. The Holy Spirit is precise in what He reveals. Nevertheless, there are things as the apostle Peter says concerning Paul, which can certainly apply to you and me as well today. Peter says,

> [*As Paul is*] speaking of this as he does in all his letters. There are some things in them hard to understand, which the ignorant and unstable twist to their own destruction, as they do the other scriptures.
>
> (2 Peter 3:16 NRS)

So, let us give careful attention to the Scripture text and especially the more difficult texts and issues. Thus, challenging each of us to pay close attention to the verse(s) at hand.

Here is how the book is laid out:

Part one is an appeal to accept all of the Bible as true and fully trustworthy. The Bible was written by men especially endowed and led by the Holy Spirit. In fact, if the Lord had not given His Word through men especially endowed and led by God, we could not know the true God or know His will.

> And that thou hast *known*[a] the holy Scriptures of a *child*, which are able to make thee wise *unto salvation*, through the faith which is in Christ *Jesus.* [16]For the whole [*all*] Scripture is *given* by inspiration of God, and is profitable to *teach*, to *convince* [*convict*], to correct, and to instruct in *righteousness.* [17]That the man of God may be absolutely [*complete*], being made perfect *unto* all good *works.*   (2 Tim. 3:15-17GNV)

> [a]Note: no words have been changed in the Geneva Bible; only the spelling is updated and the words in brackets "[ ]" are for clarity.

Peter said,

> For no prophecy was ever made by an act of human will, but men moved by the Holy Spirit spoke from God.   (2 Peter 1:21)

Jesus said,

> Heaven and earth shall pass away, but my words shall not pass away.
>
> (Matt. 24:35 KJV)

Our Lord also said concerning the authority and inspiration of the Word of God, the Bible:

> "- men to whom the word of God came (and the Scripture cannot be undone *or* annulled *or* broken)   (John 10:35 AMP)

David said by inspiration of God's Word,

> Your word, LORD, is eternal; it stands firm in the heavens
>
>   (Psa. 119:89 NIV)

Part one is a stern warning to any who rejects the Word of God. Furthermore, the warning is also sternly applied to all those who may attempt to dismiss Scripture by spiritualizing Scripture. That is, they seek to spiritualize the truth away. Such men or women have set themselves up as the final authority over the rightful authority of God's Word.

There are others who go further into dismissing Scripture by *allegorizing*. That is, they minimize the Scripture text as nothing more than some folklore or some mythology. They shall sure stand before the Lord, and their end may be worse than any nightmare ever conceived. And if they are unsaved, Hell awaits them.

There worse of the worse are those who in part or in whole reject the Scriptures. They have essentially called God a liar. Friend, declaring God a liar is indeed a most grievous sin. They deny the inspiration of Scripture as inerrantly inspired, and thus, the are actually calling the Lord a liar. Yet, the words that they declare about God and His Word are lies. Big mistake! God is holy and righteous, and He cannot lie [Titus 1:2] because He is infinitely holy and righteous. Their actions and words will come upon them as worse than a fool.

Part two, "The Lord and His Heaven is beyond description," but as to Heaven itself, God has not given any detailed description. (Though for certain He has unveiled some of the benefits or blessings in Heaven.) So, we can comprehend some of the wonderful and marvelous benefits of Heaven. As we have already noted, Heaven and all of its beauty and scenery are not permitted to be revealed at this time. There are many soothsayers, charlatans, false teachers, deluded dreamers, and liars that claimed to have gone to Heaven and come back, but they are self-deceived or liars.

There are four area we shall examine concerning our abode in Heaven. First, we shall get a glimpse into amazing "love and forgiveness." When we are in the presence of God, we may then begin to be astonished that anyone is saved because everything is so holy and righteous. For the Lord is an infinite and most holy and righteous God. We are likely to have a sense of being overwhelmed, and we marvel that anyone was saved. For example, when the beloved apostle John stood in the presence of the risen and glorified Lord Jesus Christ, the Bible says,

> [16]He had in His right hand seven stars [*Pastors*], out of His mouth went a sharp two-edged sword, and His countenance *was* like the sun shining in its strength. [17]And **when I saw Him, I fell at His feet as dead.** But He laid His right hand on me, saying to me, "Do not be afraid; I am the First and the Last. [18]"I *am* He who lives, and was dead, and behold, I am alive forevermore. Amen. And I have the keys of Hades and of Death.
>
> (Rev. 1:16-18 NKJ)

Initially in Heaven, there will be lot of crying because some of our loved-ones were not in Heaven; they are in Hell. What a shocker! Some loved-ones were in Hell because they either failed to receive the witness that some people gave to them or perhaps failed to heed the invitation to received Christ. Still others simply refused believe the Gospel. Nevertheless, in Heaven, we will be met with unceasing joy by the Lord who loves each of us with an unceasing love. As Jude says,

> Now to Him who is able to keep you from stumbling, and to make you stand in the presence of His glory blameless with great joy, to the only God our Savior, through Jesus Christ our Lord, *be* glory, majesty, dominion and authority, before all time and now and forever. Amen.
>
> (Jude 1:24, 25)

As saints in Christ, we should only desire to hear our Savior say when we meet Him, 'Well done thou good and faithful servant -' [Matt. 25:32]. Our Lord is faithful who says,

> And if anyone gives even a cup of cold water to one of these little ones who is my disciple [e.g., *believes in Jesus* Christ], truly I tell you, that person will certainly not lose their reward."　　　　(Matt. 10:42 NIV)

However, I must warn you: many people have done things through the arm of the corrupt flesh rather than the Spirit of God. So, any works in the flesh will be burned up in the fire.[1 Cor. 3:10-15]

Most shockingly, some will find out they never possessed genuine saving faith. What a shocker that will be! Some only possessed "*a profession of faith,*" but sadly, they were never truly *born from above* by the Holy Spirit. They will stand before the White Throne Judgment and shall be sent to Hell. As our Lord warns,

> Not *everyone* that saith unto me, Lord, Lord, shall enter into the kingdom of heaven; but he that doeth the will of my Father which is in heaven. [22]Many will say to me in that day, Lord, Lord, have we not prophesied in thy name? and in thy name have cast out devils? and in thy name done many wonderful works? [23]And then will I profess unto them, **I never knew you**: depart from me, ye that work iniquity.
>
> (Matt. 7:21-23 KJV)

Jesus said this is the will of God,

> [39]And this is the will of him who sent me, that I shall lose none of all those he has given me, but raise them up at the last day. [40]For my Father's **will is that everyone who LOOKS TO THE SON AND BELIEVES IN HIM SHALL HAVE ETERNAL LIFE,** and I will raise them up at the last day."
> (John 6:39, 40 NIV)

The meaning in [Matt. 7:21-23] by Jesus **IS NOT** 'I knew once, but I no longer know you.' Our statement is emphatic, '**I NEVER KNEW YOU** [*AT ANYTIME*]! **YOU WHO DO WORKS OF INIQUITY.**'

Part three: "Absence of God's Presence but only condemnation," is the shocking reality that many people shall be sent to Hell forever and ever. What a great sorrow that many missed the free gift of God, the redemption in Christ. This is because they were lost in sin, but it will be more dreadful since they heard the Gospel and yet refused the gift of God. We shall note four things concerning Hell that are so dreadful and should serve to warn anyone that rejects the Gospel. Hell is too tarrying to even contemplate, but I am here to tell plainly that awaiting the unregenerate that is outside the redemption in Christ Jesus. Therefore, believe on the Lord Jesus Christ, or else, my friend you will indeed perish in your sin in Hell without Jesus as your Redeemer.

Listen friend, Hell is the **eternal wrath of God**. We cannot even imagine the dread or terror of Hell, but even more so, who can comprehend "the eternal wrath of God?" This is infinitely worse than the wildest thoughts of humans or holy angels of God. This is wrath of God, which is without end; it is forever and ever.

We shall uncover eight false things that are (popular) but leading people to Hell. This is so serious that I have devoted two chapters to the issues; but even with two chapters, I have only skimmed the surface. What is so sorrowful in the churches today is that many Pastors, teachers, and even among the saints are no longer sharing the Gospel with the lost, and they are not giving an invitation to receive Christ as Lord. How sad is that?

The mockers of Hell (those who do not believe God's Word) have a saying, and the mockers may "laugh," and they may say to themselves, "Well, I will have a lot of company in Hell. Ha, ha!" No! In Hell, a person is all alone. Listen, Hell is described as being so dark that one cannot see their hand in front of them. They are in total isolation.

They will experience true *magnified bitterness* and *intense anger* that is unimaginable as they remain unregenerate in their old nature. Their nature as an unregenerate will not be able to change since they are void of the Holy Spirit. What is so dreadful is that their bitterness and anger will be magnified and amplified many times over.

Part four, this is "the epilogue." I will make a final plea to reexamine your profession of faith. It would be beyond belief for those who only had intellectual confession of "historical faith of fact" but void of genuine biblical saving faith in Christ. However, I am certain many went through a "canned confess" of faith in Christ, but some actually never genuinely trusted in Jesus Christ. Some will even discover they falsified or distorted God's Word, and some were led astray with their error.

Please, I beg you, listen: Heaven is real. Lord is not wanting you to perish in your sin. God is offering His infinite love right now in Christ. Our redemption was very, very costly, we are saved by shed blood and death of Jesus Christ on the cross. Yet, Heaven is free to anyone that desires to enter God's Abode, but the redemption of God is only through the Lord Jesus Christ. Here is God's promise to you, and this is a promise that comes from God who cannot lie.^{Titus 1:2}

> Because if you **CONFESS WITH YOUR MOUTH that JESUS IS LORD** and **BELIEVE IN YOUR HEART** that God raised him from the dead, **YOU WILL BE SAVED**. ¹⁰For with the heart one believes and thus **HAS RIGHTEOUSNESS** and **WITH THE MOUTH ONE CONFESSES AND THUS HAS SALVATION**. ¹¹For the scripture says, "Everyone who believes in him will not be put to shame." ¹²For there is no distinction between the Jew and the Greek, for the same Lord is Lord of all, who richly blesses all who call on him. ¹³**FOR EVERYONE WHO CALLS ON THE NAME OF THE LORD WILL BE SAVED.**   (Rom. 10:9-13 NET)

Part One

It is true, every word

CHAPTER 1

The Rude Awakening

Memory verse

"And in Hades he raised his eyes, being in torment, and saw Abraham
far away and Lazarus in his arms."   (Luke 16:23)

Introduction

Humanity has become so secularized and educated himself through the
world system that he has been desensitized to the things of God. Most regrettably, mankind has removed God from his rational thinking. Yet, others in the
world have become engulfed in every form a paganism under the sun. Still
others struggle to survive, even among some of the wealthiest countries.

Additionally, many so-called Christian churches have deliberately forsaken the Gospel and the risen Lord Jesus' mandates. Wickedness is unparalleled in many Christian churches. Yes, the wickedness is unequaled in the
history of many churches today. Immorality and every form of wickedness has
permeated *every nook and cranny* among the churches. The saints in Christ are
not even shocked or stunned at the wickedness any longer. The lack of fear and
reverence for the Lord even in the worship service is unbelievably appalling.
There is no fear of God. So, many have turned themselves into "fools."

Please let me warn you and I beg you to hear me, there are irrefutable signs
of Christ's return. The world and many of the saints are seemingly oblivious to
these blatant signs. Wake up my friend, our Lord's coming maybe sooner than
you might imagine.

Consider the following signs. First, God is *summing Israel* back in the
promised land in Israel. The nation of Israel is becoming an awesome power in

1

their own right world-wide. In addition, the HEB language had been dead for two thousand years, but now, the *HEB language has been completely revived*. Wow, who has heard or thought of such a thing? Amazingly, even the *temple in Jerusalem is on the verge of construction*. The priests are completely trained for priestly service, and even the altar for sacrifices has been already fully consecrated under the Mosaic Law.

There are still other signs. *War and destruction* are on edge. The world is like mighty powder keg really to blow up. For example, man has created nuclear weapons so frightening and terrifying it could destroy all life as we know it everywhere. Keep in mind, there are crazy leaders in the world that are foolish enough to use such awesome weaponry if they had it. The tensions are so great in some places in the world there is *little peace among certain nations*. Believe me, some countries are on edge. The *threat of a global holocaust war* is a frightening possibility.

Artificial intelligence (AI) is making quantum leaps at staggering speed. The speed with which AI is progressing is *alarming* to say the least. AI is expanding exponentially faster than most of humankind can even imagine. It sounds like a science fiction thriller, but this is real, friend, and not make-believe. Listen, humanoid robots are already here.

There are yet more unbelievable signs that our Lord's coming is very near. *Asteroids are now falling* on the earth (the Bible calls them stars). Some of these asteroids are very large and could cause incalculable devastation and destruction. There are many *earthquakes, dreadful famines, pestilence*, and the *dread of diseases* in some parts of the world. There is the possibility of alarming *global warming*.

In addition, much of the earth's *natural resources are depleted* in some places. And to top it off, *pollution of earth* and its effects upon all life is very alarming and is a very serious problem. There is the *deterioration of the ozone* around the earth, which could greatly jeopardize life. *Water is being severely contaminated* in some places, and sometimes even becoming poisonous. Even the *air we breathe is becoming toxic* in portions of the world.

So, what does all of this mean to humankind? Friend, I warn you; we may be closer to the *Parousia*[1] than anyone dare imagine. I am referring particularly to our Lord coming to judge the world in righteousness. I am not referring to the rapture of the church, which come prior to Parousia. The Parousia is indeed the most terrifying and horrifying day since man first walk upon the earth.

Our Lord said,

²¹For then there will be a great tribulation, such as has not occurred since the beginning of the world until now, nor ever will *again*. ²²And if those days had not been cut short, no life would have been saved; but for the sake of the elect those days will be cut short. ²³Then if anyone says to you, 'Behold, here is the Christ,' or '*He is over* here,' do not believe *him*. ²⁴For false christs and false prophets will arise and will provide great signs and wonders, so as to mislead, if possible, even the elect. ²⁵Behold, I have told you in advance.   (Matt. 24:21-25)

Jesus continues by saying,

"Immediately after the tribulation of those days the sun will be darkened, and the moon will not give its light, and the stars will fall from heaven, and the powers of the heavens will be shaken. ³⁰**Then will appear in heaven THE SIGN of the Son of Man**, and then all the tribes of the earth will mourn, and **they will see the Son of Man coming on the clouds of heaven** with power and great glory." (Matt. 24:29, 30 ESV)

The bulk of the professing theological world alleges that Jesus' prophecy has been fulfilled in 70 AD by Titus and the Roman Army. (This is when Titus' Army leveled Jerusalem, and the Army did not leave one stone unturned.) Jesus' prophecy of total destruction is yet to be fulfilled. So, friend, actually the above prophecies are now coming ever closer to being fulfilled and fully realized. Woe unto the world when this Day is realized.

A. "I would have never believed it!"

This is the shocking truth to be literally realized. People in that moment shall not understand what is happening in the world around them. Ironically, people will be saying to themselves, 'I would have never believed it!' Their own self-realization is the admission that they would not have believed it even if many reliable witnesses had told them the truth of faith in Christ and our Lord's terrifying return in fury and His wrath.

People will be thrusted into the greatest tribulation the world has ever known. This is one of the worse prophesies event in the annals of human history of the world. Due to mankind's ignorance, unbelief, callused hearts, and the mesmerizing and magnetic illustration of the world, humanity has become blinded to truth of **Jesus' free gift of eternal life**. As a result, man has turned a *deaf ear* to the warning of the dreadful coming of Jesus Christ and His return to judge the world in righteousness.

The saints in Christ need to wake up to the apostle Paul's warning,

3

This is why it is said: "**Wake up**, sleeper, rise from the dead, and Christ will shine on you." [15]Be very careful, then, how you live— not as unwise but as wise, [16]making the most of every opportunity, because the days are evil. [17] Therefore do not be foolish, but understand what the Lord's will is. [18]Do not get drunk on wine, which leads to debauchery. Instead, be filled with the Spirit, [19]speaking to one another with psalms, hymns, and songs from the Spirit. Sing and make music from your heart to the Lord. (Eph. 5:14-19 NIV)

The saints are first in line for judgment. Unfortunately, there are many churches that are spiritually asleep today. The apostle Peter says very plainly,

For the time *is come* that judgment must begin at the house of God: and if *it* first *begin* at us, what shall the end *be* of them that obey not the gospel of God? And if the righteous scarcely be saved, where shall the ungodly and the sinner appear? (1 Peter 4:17, 18 KJV)

Please listen to me my friend! If I am understanding Peter correctly, the saints will be the first in line to be examined by the Lord for their faithfulness. (The believers are not examined for salvation; they will be examined as to faithfulness and service.) Is Peter alluding to the rapture? If the apostle is, he may have in mind the church is raptured of Christians prior to judgment the world which we noted above. (However, the unsaved will be judged at the **Great White Throne Judgment**.[Rev. 20:10-15]) However, Peter is likely referring to the **Judgment [*Bema*] Seat of God**,[2 Cor. 5:10] which has to do with *rewards* or *loss of rewards*.

Listen to me my brother, the judgment of the saints will not be *chit chat* or a *walk through tulips*. Pay close attention again as Peter says,

— if it [*the judgment of God*] begins with us [*the saved*], what will the outcome be for those who do not obey the gospel of God? And, "If it is hard [GK *molos, difficulty* or *scarcely*] for the righteous [a]to be saved, what will become of the ungodly and the sinner?" (1 Peter 4:17, 18 NIV)

[a]Note: this is the imputed righteousness we received through genuine faith in Christ Jesus through the Holy Spirit, [Rom. 8:30 1 Cor. 1:30; 6:11]. The Bible is clear *there is no righteous, no not one.*[Ecc. 7:20; Rom. 3:10]

Yes, and amen, the door is open to all that will believe and receive Christ Jesus as Lord and Savior. Nevertheless, Lord Jesus warns that if anyone refuses to believe in Him, that person has condemned himself. The unbeliever remains under the wrath of God, and that person will indeed die in their sins.[John 3:18, 36; 8:24] Yet, while the door to eternal life in Heaven is open to everyone that wants to genuinely receive Jesus as Lord and Savior, He emphatically warns,

> "Enter through the narrow gate; for the gate is wide and the way is broad that leads to destruction, and there are many who enter through it. For the gate is small and the way is narrow that leads to life, and there are few who find it." (Matt. 7:13, 14)

Jesus continues and warns,

> [21]"Not everyone who says to Me, 'Lord, Lord,' shall enter the kingdom of heaven, but he who does the will of My Father in heaven. [22]"Many will say to Me in that day, 'Lord, Lord, have we not prophesied[b] in Your name, cast out demons in Your name, and done many wonders in Your name?' [23]"And then I will declare to them, '**I NEVER KNEW YOU**; depart from Me, you who practice lawlessness!' (Matt. 7:21-23 NKJ)

> [b]Note: the person is relying on his "religious deeds" to somehow justify their righteousness. However, eternal life is a "free gift" through genuine saving faith in Christ and being born from above by the sanctifying work of the Holy Spirit.

Jesus warns many people will miss the **free gift of God**, eternal life through faith in Him. They missed the gift of God because they sought Heaven based on their so-called good works or religious rites rather than through personal commitment and saving faith in and through Jesus Christ and His redemption on the cross. Many failed to make the commitment and trust in Jesus Christ's work and His sacrifice on Calvary. The apostle Paul is explicit that redemption is the work of God; redemption is not humankind's religious works or religious rites,

> For the wages of sin is death, but the **FREE GIFT OF GOD** is eternal life in Christ Jesus our Lord. (Rom. 6:23)

What travesty, many people have been blinded by their own religious prejudice. Yes, people have been blinded by their own religious prejudice. You got it: their own bigotry caused them to miss the Gospel. How sad is that? Like Judas Iscariot who betrayed Jesus, many people missed the *greatest gift of God* due to manmade religion, which might be referred to as *religiousology*.

How can anyone miss the wonderful gift of God? Religion, regardless of what form it is, declares that you must have good works to get into Heaven. Friend, you cannot earn your way into Heaven. (What kind Heaven is that where man can boast of his work?) Neither is Heaven attained by works plus faith. We enter Heaven solely through faith in Christ, and friend, it is all by grace and grace alone.

> [15]We *who are* Jews by nature, and not sinners of the Gentiles, [16]knowing that a man is not justified [*righteous*] [c]by the works of the law but by faith in Jesus Christ, even we have believed [*trusted*] in Christ Jesus, that we might be justified [*righteous*] by faith in Christ and not by the works of the law; for by the works of the law no flesh shall be justified [*righteous*].

> [19]"For I through the law died to the law that I might live to God. [20]I have been crucified with Christ; it is no longer I who live, but Christ lives in me; and the *life* which I now live in the flesh I live by faith in [*of*] the Son of God, who loved me and gave Himself for me. [21]I do not set aside [*invalid*] the grace of God; **for if righteousness *comes* through the law, then Christ died in vain.**" (Gal. 2:15, 16, 19-21)

> [c]Note: the word "*justified*" is the same word "righteous" in ENG. That is, we are made righteous through genuine faith by trust Christ Jesus' work on the cross. For example, see 2 Cor. 5:21; Phi. 3:9.

The NET is may be closer in meaning, though KJV is close. The NET reads this way in Galatians verse 20, "I live because **of the faithfulness of the Son of God,** who loved me and gave himself for me."[Gal. 2:19 NET]

Friend, listen to me! Do not end up in Hell[2] and saying to yourself, 'I would have never believed it!' Eternal life is free to everyone that genuinely places their complete trust and commitment in Jesus Christ as Lord and Savior. No one needs to go to Hell. Ask the Lord to make Himself plain to you, and friend, He will make Himself plainly known to you. However, you must receive Jesus as Lord and be born from above through genuinely receiving and trusting the Lord Jesus today. Don't delay.

B. "If I had only listened and believed God's Word"

"*The Rude Awakening*" will comes as some people with scathing scorn and saying to themselves, *If I had only listened and believed God's Word.* Why do I say, "*scathing scorn*?" This is because in Hell, they remain in their unregenerate nature. The unsaved (those unregenerate) remain in old nature and unchanged and unable to change. The unsaved are sadly totally void of any goodness, love, mercy, grace that comes from God. So, unregenerate, they are incapable of repenting. Hence, they can only be *filled with rage* and *full of bitterness*. This is the actual portrait or picture we get of the rich man in Hades awaiting the final judgment. But friend, this is what our true natural is before we were sanctified and indwelt by Spirit of God.[Titus 3:3ff]

You see my friend, without the grace of God and possessing a new nature from the Holy Spirit, man cannot change. This is the difference between *religion* which is <u>manmade</u> *over against* true <u>saving</u> <u>grace</u> in the risen Lord and Savior Jesus Christ. *Religion is from below*. Religion's inception is from man's carnal and depraved mind. Whereas, genuine saving faith in Jesus Christ *is from above*, and salvation given by the Spirit of the living God. Hallelujah!

Salvation is **not a reformation** through so-called religion and changing one's self. Salvation is God purchasing His redeemed. Get it right: redemption is the power of God and His redeeming and cleansing grace working within the genuine believer. Hello! The **Lord paid for our redemption** through the Son of God dying in the place of (*on behalf of*) the believers. Christ Jesus died in my place on the cross, and He died in your place on the cross if you are truly saved. Jesus died for all genuine believers on the cross. Our Lord bore the sins of all true believers in His own body.[1 Peter 1:18, 19; 2:24] The Lord Jesus Christ became *a vicarious substitute* in our place for our sins.

Jesus *propitiated* our sin. Meaning that Jesus dying on the cross for our sin *satisfied*, *placated*, and *appeased* the wrath of God for every believer. Listen, we must understand Christ did not just die on behalf the sins of the believers; our Lord died in the place of the believer. So, He died in my place for sin and He died in your place for sin in payment for your sin. Christ the Lord died taking the sinners place and received the wrath God on his behalf. In exchange for genuine saving faith in Christ (trusting in Christ as Lord), God has by His grace imputed the very righteousness of Christ to every true believer.[2 Cor. 5:21] Hence, we stand complete in Him.[Col. 2:9, 10]

Watch out: there are many that may claim to be Christians, but they shall unfortunately discover that their alleged faith was in religion. Their faith was **not** actually relying in Jesus' sacrifice for sin on the cross. For example, many religions allege that water baptism by a religious leader washes away sin or even that religious works justifies a person before God. Thus, canceling out Jesus' sacrifice for sin on the cross, and making His sacrifice for sin insufficient for salvation. This is a blatant ecclesiastical fabricated lie.

Others who profess faith in Christ only possess an *historical faith*, an intellectual acknowledgment without personally trusting the Lord Jesus. Yes, they only acknowledge the historical fact of Calvary but without truly placing their trust in Him. Intellectually, they may believe the Gospel to be true. However, they had **never** made a <u>genuine</u> <u>commitment</u> and <u>full</u> <u>reliance</u> in Christ's sufficiency on the cross. They had **never** personally called upon the Lord Jesus to be their Lord and Savior. Yet, the Bible plainly tells us,

> Because if you **confess with your mouth** that Jesus is Lord **AND believe in your heart** that God raised him from the dead, you will be saved. [10]For **with the heart one believes** and **thus has righteousness** and **with the mouth one confesses and thus has salvation**. [11]For the scripture says, "Everyone who believes in him will not be put to shame." [12]For there is no distinction between the Jew and the Greek, for the same Lord is Lord of all, who richly blesses all who call on him. [13]**For everyone who calls on the name of the Lord will be saved**.
>
> (Rom. 10:9-13 NET)

Let us avoid reading more in the Scriptures than is implied. There are people that believed and confessed in their *inner-being* because they may be mute and dumb and unable to openly confess Christ. That is, they may have been unable to speak or even hear. So, a person does not necessarily have to speak verbally or audibly in words. The Lord reads the heart and mind. 'I am He who searches [*examines*] the minds and hearts.'[Rev. 2:23 NKJ] So, there are people who may have made a confession of faith in Christ in their heart. Yet, there others that remain unregenerate though they confessed Christ audibly it was not coupled with genuine saving faith. There are people that may be mute or dumb (cannot speak or hear) who believed and confessed the faith in their minds or hearts. Yet, their confession of faith occurred in their minds, and they were truly saved.

Again, Scripture says,

> But to all who have **received him**– those who **believe in his name**– he has given the right [GK *exousia, legitimate authority*] to become God's children[d]– children not born by human parents or by human desire or a husband's decision, but by God. (John 1:12, 13 NET)

[d]Note: the GK word [in v 12] is **not** son; the GK word is "*teknon*," children.

The bottom line (*the conclusion of the matter*) there will be people in Hell remembering that they had the opportunity to believe God and His Word, the Bible, but they missed the Gospel because they **refused** to believe or trust in Jesus as Lord. Trusting is such a simple action, but the arrogant or egotistic denied trusting Jesus as Lord is all it takes to be saved.

I had a secular professor psychologist at a college who did not believe the Bible, and he said to me, "Well, I do not believe one goes to Heaven simply by believing in Jesus Christ." He set himself up as final authority. Whether or not the professor believed there was Hell, I do not know. There is one thing for sure, there will be no denying the existence of Hell in the Lake of Fire! By that I mean, Hell will be fully realized as an unbeliever sits in Hell. Sadly also, the unbelieving profession of faith was not a genuine possession of genuine saving faith in Christ. He had a different Jesus and a different Gospel. Jesus paid for all our sins on the cross. Hallelujah!

Conclusion

The Rude Awakening is indeed coming as Jesus said, 'For the gate is small and the way is narrow that leads to life, **AND THERE ARE FEW WHO FIND IT**.'Matt. 7:14 Friend, *the Rude Awaking* is coming. Do not let your loved-ones perish and wake up in Hell. Heaven is real, and yes, Hell is real. There is no reason for anyone to be in Hell especially since God so loved the world. Regrettably, there will be many in Hell that shall realize they missed the free gift of God because they did not believe God or His Word.

> For God so loved the world, that he gave his only begotten Son, that whosoever believeth in him should not perish, but have everlasting life. 17For God sent not his Son into the world to condemn the world; but that the world through him might be saved. 18He that believeth on him is not condemned: but he that believeth not is condemned already, because he hath not believed in the name of the only begotten Son of God.
>
> (John 3:16-18 KJV)

The churches are disobeying the risen Lord Jesus' mandates. The churches are failing to give the Gospel and invitation to receive Christ as Lord and Savior. The churches are failing to warn the people they must repent. People must come to Jesus now while there is still time. The door to Heaven is open to everyone that is willing come right now.

But everyone must come through Jesus; He is the only One that can save us from our sins. There is no religion that can save us from our sins. Salvation is only through Jesus Christ that is able to save us from our sins. There is no religious institution or church that can save us from our sins. Only Christ the Lord saves. There is no religious act, such as water baptism, that saves us from our sin. Only Jesus Christ's shed blood and death at Calvary can save us.

Jesus Christ our Lord gives this promise to everyone that genuinely commits their life and personally trust and receives Him today,

> Truly, truly, I tell you, whoever hears My word and believes Him who sent Me has eternal life and **WILL NOT COME UNDER JUDGMENT**. Indeed, **HE HAS CROSSED OVER FROM DEATH TO LIFE**. (John 5:24 MSB)

Will you trust Jesus as Lord and receive the free gift of eternal life right now, today?

> For the wages of sin is death, but the free gift of God is eternal life in Christ Jesus our Lord. (Rom. 6:23)

Footnotes

1. *Parousia*: is a GK word for *coming* or *arrival* of our Lord. *Parousia* is one of the words that describes the coming of the Lord Jesus. This is a very important biblical word, though there are also other words in the Bible used to describe our Lord's coming.

2. Hell: this is the common word or usual word for the final abode of wicked. That is, people refer to the final place of the lost as Hell. Actually, the word hell in the Bible: OT common HEB word is *Sheol* and in the NT GK word is *Hades*. Another word is the GK word *Tartaros*. *Tartaros* may be the present temporary abode and waiting the final judgment of certain evil angels that went too far in their transgression. These evil angels had to be confined. Some evil angels just went too far in rebellion. These evil angels' final abode is actually the *Lake of Fire*, which is the final abode of unsaved.[Rev. 20:15]

    The Bible tells us, "And death and hell (GK Hades) were cast into the lake of fire. This is the second death."[Rev. 20:14 KJV] The phrase "And death and Hades" may be a HEB (OT) implying "death and the *grave*." The abode of souls/spirits in Hades awaiting the judgment. However, the unregenerate's body will be raised and united with their soul/spirit to stand at Judgement and be cast into Hell alive forever.

    The KJV is literally correct, "- and they lived and reigned with Christ a thousand years."[Rev. 20:4 KJV] There are some that may think Hades is only referring the grave; in which case, there is similarity between death and grave.[e.g. 1 Cor 15:54-55] Note the parallel below where <u>Hades</u> is translated <u>grave</u> by KJV. This a quote from Isaiah 25:8, but the HEB is "*maveth*." "*Maveth*" means <u>death</u> and **not** *Sheol* or *Hades* (*grave*.) The ASV is the preferred meaning.

So when this corruptible shall have put on incorruption, and this mortal shall have put on immortality, then shall be brought to pass the saying that is written, Death is swallowed up in victory. O death, where *is* thy sting? O grave [BYZ GK *hades*], where *is* thy victory? 1 Cor 15:54, 55 KJV	But when this corruptible shall have put on incorruption, and this mortal shall have put on immortality, then shall come to pass the saying that is written, Death is swallowed up in victory. O death, where is thy victory? O death [Other GK *thanatos*, lit. *death*], where is thy sting? 1 Cor. 15:54, 55 ASV

As noted above, Paul quotes Isaiah with final blessing of the redeemed with the Lord in Heaven with the risen and glorified bodies,

He will swallow up death[e] in victory; and the Lord GOD will wipe away tears from off all faces; and the rebuke of his people shall he take away from off all the earth: for the LORD hath spoken *it*.

(Isa. 25:8 KJV)

[e]Note: the "*death*" is the HEB *maveth* which is the OT LXX (GK) *thanatos*, which is lit. "death." Hence, older manuscript supports the word **death** rather than *grave* or *hades*. So, Paul is referring to death and not the grave or hades.

CHAPTER 2

Death is the final Commencement

Memory verse

But God said to him, 'You fool! This *very* night your soul is demanded of you; and *as for all* that you have prepared, who will own *it now?*'

(Luke 12:20)

Introduction

I suppose many assume that at death, "It will be all over." (They are no longer in existence once they have died.) Whether a person lived a wicked life, or lived a modest, good life, or even if some lived a life of suffering; it is all over now. Perhaps, "He/she rests in peace now." There is no resting in peace, that is a misnomer.

The above is a very nice *platitude of words* at a person's gravesite or committal service. This is however not really what happens at death. God's Word declares there are two doors at death that lead into eternity. At death, the person enters into the door they have chosen. As we enter that door of choice, this is indeed the final Commencement. This is the person's beginning into his eternal abode. That is, a person either makes their final commitment for Heaven, or they made the final commitment for Hell, even if that decision for Hell is made by default.[1]

I imagine that some people might mockingly think within themselves (though they do not believe in Hell) "Hey, I am not making a commitment to Hell!" My friend, I am here to tell you that if you **do not** make a commitment

13

and trust in Jesus Christ today, you have by default made an eternal commitment to enter an everlasting Hell.

I am not trying to scare you out of Hell into Heaven. This is not the method of the Gospel. Friend, God is _extending_ or _offering_ you His infinite love, mercy, and grace right now through Jesus Christ our Lord. The Lord wants to be your loving and very best Friend today. Moreover, the Lord our God wants to be your very best Friend throughout eternity.

To be His friend, you must come through Jesus Christ right now while there is still time. The Word of God is very plain: there is no other name but Jesus that can save you or anyone else from their sins right now, today. You must come to Jesus as your Lord and Savior, and He will indeed make you a citizen of His Heaven right now, today.

> "And there is salvation in no one else; for there is no other name under heaven that has been given among mankind by which we must be saved."
> (Acts 4:12)

Please listen to me friend and do not delay, the Bible is very, very clear, "-behold, now _is_ the accepted time; behold, now _is_ the day of salvation."[2 Cor. 6:2 KJV] If you delay or put off making the decision for Jesus, Hell awaits you. Friend, realize this that your delay is actually saying, **"NO TO JESUS."** Whether you realize it or not, you are rejecting His love He is offering you by not making a decision. Don't say, "No, to yourself." God's Word says very clearly,

> "Whoever believes in him is not condemned, but **whoever does not believe stands condemned already** because they have not believed in the name of God's one and only Son."
> (John 3:18 NIV)

Furthermore, the Bible continues with this concluding statement,

> "He who believes in the Son has everlasting life; and he who does not believe the Son shall not see life, but the wrath of God abides on him."
> (John 3:36 NKJ)

Listen to me friend, the Lord has made a commitment to save you today if you will choose eternal life with Jesus as Lord. However, if you fail to choose to repent and trust Jesus right now, your answer is no to the Lord and Savior who came to save you from your sins. Remember this, if you fail to make decision for Christ Jesus as Lord, then you have made a decision to enter Hell by default. That is, make no decision, and you have made the decision by default to place yourself into Hell.

That is, wait until death, then, you shall indeed stand before the Lord. Standing before the Lord your God, you remain under the wrath of God forever and condemned. There will be no appeal. You have condemned yourself to an eternal Hell. Friend, how sad is that?

A. You make the Commitment

Friend, I am warning you the best way I know how. I am telling you that *there is no cop out* by saying that you did not make a decision. Your delay is the rejection of God's offer of redemption. Making no decision, you have made the decision. Do you understand what I mean? Your decision was, "No to the Lord Jesus." Saying nothing or doing nothing! You are actually saying, "No to His free gift eternal life in Him."[Rom. 6:23] Listen, do not be foolish and make no decision because your indecisiveness will put you in Hell.

Yes, your indecisiveness will put you into an eternal Hell. Friend, this is like boarding "*Jesus' bus*;" He is the only one that can take you to Heaven. But you have to get on-board with Jesus right now, today. Here is the Good News, repent and receive Jesus Christ as your Lord and Savior, and He will make you a citizen of Heaven right now, today.

The Bible tells us that when we make a genuine commitment and trust in Jesus Christ as Lord and Savior, we are made us citizens of Heaven immediately, today:

> But our **citizenship IS in heaven**– and we also await a *Savior* from there, the Lord Jesus Christ, who will transform these humble bodies of ours into the likeness of his glorious body by means of that power by which he is able to subject all things to himself.   (Phil. 3:20, 21 NET)

Do you see it? If you genuinely repent and trust in Jesus as Lord and Savior- "—**our citizenship IS in heaven** -." This happens the moment you personally turn to Jesus as Lord and Savior. Do you recall the promise we read in the previous chapter? The Bible gives us this sure promise as plainly given by Amplified Bible,

> But to as many as did receive *and* welcome Him [*Jesus as Lord*], He gave the right [the authority, the privilege] to become children of God, *that is,* to those who believe in (adhere to, trust in, and rely on) His name— who were born, not of blood [natural conception], nor of the will of the flesh [physical impulse], nor of the will of man [that of a natural father], but of God [that is, a divine and supernatural birth--they are born of God-- spiritually transformed, renewed, sanctified].   (John 1:12, 13 AMP)

15

What am I saying to you? Well, if you want to be in Heaven, then, **you must make your commitment to trust and receive** Jesus as Lord and Savior right now, today. Friend, this is not just intellectually believing the fact that Jesus died for our sins and arose again on the third day and is coming back. This is only *historical faith*; this is only acknowledging the truth of the Gospel. This is the deadly error of religion. Faith is personally making the commitment and inviting Christ to come and redeem you from your sin. Your need to make Jesus Christ the Lord and only Sovereign over your life. We must genuinely trust in Jesus. When Jesus owns you as Lord and Savior, He owns you *"lock, stock, and barrel."* If you refuse trust and receive Jesus, then, I am telling you that you will surely perish without Christ. He owns you if truly trust Him. You cannot be delivered from your sins and rescued from Hell without make the personal commitment and trust.

> Flee sexual immorality. Every sin that a man does is outside the body, but he who commits sexual immorality sins against his own body. ¹⁹Or do you not know that your body is the temple of the Holy Spirit *who is* in you, whom you have from God, and **you are not your own?** ²⁰**For you were bought at a price**; therefore glorify God in your body and in your spirit, which are God's.   (1 Cor. 6:18-20 NKJ)

You have to make the choice. You must call upon the Lord Jesus as your personal Lord and Savior and make a definite commitment. Intellectually believing the fact is **not** truly genuine saving faith in Christ. Believing the fact proves you not stupid. You must personally call upon the Lord Jesus out of a genuine and true heart of faith. Do you remember what the apostle said in Romans 10 concerning saving faith? Let me refresh your memory, and let us look at it from the NIV:

> If you declare with your mouth, "Jesus is Lord," and **BELIEVE IN YOUR HEART** that God raised him from the dead, you will be saved. ¹⁰For it is with your heart that you believe and are justified, and it is **WITH YOUR MOUTH THAT YOU PROFESS YOUR FAITH AND ARE SAVED.** ¹¹As Scripture says, "Anyone who believes in him will never be put to shame." ¹²For there is no difference between Jew and Gentile— the same Lord is Lord of all and richly blesses all who call on him, ¹³for, **"EVERYONE WHO CALLS ON THE NAME OF THE LORD WILL BE SAVED."**   (Rom. 10:9-13 NIV)

Friend, if you are hurting inside spiritually and feeling unworthy, talk to the Lord out loud or with your mind or heart. As I have said, you do not have to confess audibly. You can silently pray in your heart. Praying silently, this is the same as confessing with your mouth. The Lord Jesus hears your faint cry of your heart and mind. He is standing by right now ready to receive you as a son or daughter into the Kingdom of God. Read the Scripture again [Rom. 10:9-13] and call upon the Lord Jesus by faith right now. He reads your heart and mind just same as if you confess with your mouth that Christ Jesus is Lord out loud. The Lord will indeed forgive you of all your sin. Yes, and praise the Lord, He will make you His child forever. He will do it right now, today. Will you call upon Him right now to save you?

The Lord Jesus Christ is inviting you into His Kingdom. His invitation is through genuine saving faith in His redemption that He accomplished on the cross. Do you want to receive the free gift of God, eternal life through Jesus Christ? Then, you must personally call upon Him. Repent and confessing that you are a sinner on the road to Hell. Confess that you want to make the commitment and fully put your trust in Him as Lord and Savior. Confessing that you believe Jesus died for your sins and arose the third day and is coming back. You are asking to receive the Lord Jesus as your personal Lord and Savior right now, today.

Friend, I know this true. I personally made that commitment at nine years old. I made that commitment during a most unlike time. My commitment was given during dismissal of junior department at the close of Sunday School. It was very noisy every one moving around, but it suddenly became quiet. I could not believe how quiet it was even with the children moving around. I heard very clearly the invitation to receive the Lord Jesus. I made the commitment that day, and praise the Lord, I was saved. Jesus has been the greatest Friend I have. He will be your greatest Friend too if you will invite Jesus to be your Lord and Savior right now, today.

B. The Burden rests on you

Neither your Dad nor Mom nor your grandparents can make your decision for you. Water baptism, church membership, or religious affiliation cannot give you eternal life. You cannot earn your way into Heaven. Eternal life is given as **free gift of God** but only through Jesus Christ as Lord and Savior.[Rom. 6:23]

Pay attention: if you want be in Heaven, then, I am telling you right now that the burden of going to Heaven rests on you. Let me also tell you that if you have the slightest doubt concerning whether you made a genuine commitment to Jesus Christ as Lord and Savior, then, please make sure right now, make the

17

commitment right now. The Bible encourages each person to reexamine their confession of faith in Christ. Reexamine your faith to determine whether you are saved or not. The Bible says,

> Test *and* evaluate yourselves *to see* whether you are in the faith *and* living your lives as [committed] believers. Examine yourselves [not me[a]]! Or do you not recognize this about yourselves [by an ongoing experience] that Jesus Christ is in you—unless indeed you fail the test *and* are rejected as counterfeit? (2 Cor. 13:5 AMP)

> [a]Note: AMP add or inserts the words "[*not me*]" because some Corinthians were questioning Paul's authority as an apostle.

The Amplified Bible is like a paraphrase translation, but the Amplified is close to the intended meaning of Paul. No one will fail the test if they genuinely call upon Jesus as Lord to be their personal Redeemer.

> For I have come down from heaven not to do my will but to do the will of him who sent me. [39]And this is the will of him who sent me, that **I SHALL LOSE NONE** of all those he has given me, but raise them up at the last day. [40]For my Father's will is that **everyone who looks to the Son and BELIEVES IN HIM SHALL HAVE ETERNAL LIFE**, and I will raise them up at the last day." (John 6:38-40 NIV)

Watch out for the cults that would mislead.

In the above text [John 6:38-40], Jesus is referring particularly to the resurrection of the physical body. This is because at death the soul of person will either enter Heaven or Hades. Everyone that truly trusts in Christ will go immediately to Heaven at death. However, the soul that is without Christ as their personal Redeemer shall immediately go to Hades. In Hades, they await the Judgment. Then, the unregenerate soul shall be united with the body and stand before the Judge and be sentenced to Hell, the Lake of Fire.

The Bible says concerning those redeemed in Christ at death that they will be present with the Lord Jesus in Heaven.

> We are confident, *I say*, and willing rather to be absent from the body, and to be present with the Lord. (2 Cor. 5:8 KJV)

Again, the apostle says of his own concern at death,

> For to me to live is Christ, and to die is gain. [22]If I am to live in the flesh, that means fruitful labor for me. Yet which I shall choose I cannot tell.

[23]I am hard pressed between the two. My desire is to depart and be with Christ, for that is far better. (Phi. 1:21-23 ESV)

As to the souls being in Heaven, the Lord Jesus rebuked and corrected the Sadducees who did not believe in eternal life and denied the resurrection of the body. Jesus said,

[29]Jesus answered and said to them, "You are mistaken, not knowing the Scriptures nor the power of God. [30]For in the resurrection they neither marry nor are given in marriage, but are like angels of God in heaven. [31]But concerning the resurrection of the dead, have you not read what was spoken to you by God, saying, [32]'**I am the God of Abraham, the God of Isaac, and the God of Jacob'? God is not the God of the dead, but of the living**." (Matt. 22:29-32 NKJ)

Jesus meant that the saints are very much alive in their souls in Heaven upon death. This is why we read of those who have been martyred for their faith in Christ that they are in Heaven and asking the Lord Jesus Christ,

[9]When *the Lamb* broke the fifth seal, **I saw underneath the altar the souls** of those who had been killed because of [*their faith in*] the *Word* of God, and because of the testimony which they had maintained; [10]and **they cried out with a loud voice**, saying, "How long, O Lord, holy and true, will You refrain from judging and avenging our blood on those who live on the earth?" [11]And a **white robe was given to each of them**; and they were told that they were to rest for a little while longer, until *the number of* their fellow servants and their brothers *and sisters* who were to be killed even as they *had been*, was completed also. (Rev. 6:9-11)

So, the Bible is clear that the saints, the believers, are in Heaven awaiting transformation of their body.[Rom. 8:22, 23; Phi. 3:20, 21] Remember Enoch and Elijah went directly to Heaven in their physical bodies which were gloriously transformed as they left this world.[Gen 5:21-24 (Heb. 11:5); 2 Kings 2:11]

However, we shall indeed reign in our physical bodies with Christ on earth. (What an unusual paradox? Some with resurrected bodies and perhaps ambassador of Heaven, but there are others in natural bodies.) The Bible tell us,

And I saw thrones, and they sat upon them, and judgment was given unto them: and *I saw* the souls of them that were beheaded for the witness of Jesus, and for the word of God, and which had not worshipped the beast, neither his image, neither had received *his* mark upon their foreheads, or in their hands; and **they lived**[b] **and reigned with Christ a thousand years**. (Rev. 20:4 KJV) ᵇNote: (as remarked earlier) the KJV and ASV are literally correct here in the GK text. Some newer translations incorrectly add "and they came to life." There is **no** such phrase in the GK text here. The phrase is unwarranted insertion. The souls of the saints were already alive in Heaven, but now the saints' souls are united with their body in the resurrection. So, the saints **DID NOT** "and they came to life;" the saints were alive in their souls.

Still, the burden rests on you. Your parent or grandparent cannot make the decision of faith in Christ for you. There are no grandchildren in the faith. You must be born from above by the Spirit of God through personal saving faith in Jesus as Lord. Eternal life in Christ is your choice to make. Remember, if you **make no decision**, you have indeed made the decision to reject Jesus Christ.

The apostle John warns us,

(The one who believes in the Son of God has the testimony in himself; the one who does not believe God has made him a liar, because he has not believed in the testimony that God has testified concerning his Son.) ¹¹And this is the testimony: God has given us eternal life, and this [*eternal*] life is in his Son. ¹²The one who has the Son has this eternal life; the one who does not have the Son of God does not have this eternal life. ¹³I have written these things to you who believe in the name of the Son of God so that you may know that you have eternal life.   (1 John 5:10-13 NET)

Friend, if you do not recall calling upon Jesus making a personal commitment and genuine trust in the Lord Jesus, you need to carefully reexamine your confession of faith. Remember, Jesus said,

"Most assuredly, I say to you, he who hears My word and believes in Him who sent Me has everlasting life, and shall not come into judgment, but [*he that trust in Christ*] **has passed from death into life**." (John 5:24 NKJ)

My question to you is, "Do you remember when you '*has passed from death into life*?'" Friend, if you do not recall when you called upon the Lord to save you from you sins and ask for eternal life in Christ, you are indeed on shaky ground.

Also, saving faith is **not** just believing the historical facts that Jesus died for your sin and arose again (as already noted earlier). You must make a personal commitment to completely place your trust in Jesus' sacrifice on the cross for your sins.

Therefore, understand that the burden truly rests on you to make the personal decision for Christ. You are the only one that can take that step to faith. Repent of your sins right now. Declare unwaveringly that you want to make the commitment at this moment. You want to put your full trust and complete reliance that the Lord Jesus died on the cross for you sins and arose the third day. And right now by faith you want to receive Him as your personal Lord and Savior.

Here is God's promise, and this is a promise that comes from the Lord our God who cannot lie.^{Titus 1:2}

> For whosoever shall call upon the name of the Lord shall be saved.
>
> (Rom. 10:13 KJV)

Call upon right now, and Jesus will indeed save you.

Conclusion

Do not listen to the lie of the world that says, "Death ends all." Death is the final Commencement! There are two doors into eternity. One door is into Heaven, and this is forever and ever. This where we shall spend eternity in Presence of a holy and righteous God who loves us.

The other door leads to Hell. There is no return. There is no second chance. All who refuse to repent and receive Jesus as Lord and Savior are on a one-way ticket into Hell.

In Heaven, *God shall wipe away our tears.*^{Rev. 21:4} Why will the Lord *wipe away the tears from our eye?* This is because some people actually did not believe the Gospel. Others, while they professed to believe, they never made the personal commitment and trusting Jesus sacrifice for sins. They only had historical faith without the personal commitment and trust in Jesus as Lord and only Savior.

Therefore, my friend, *you must make the commitment.* Listen, no one else can make that commitment for you. You must be born again from above by the Spirit of God through a genuine commitment and trust in Jesus. Otherwise, I regret to tell you that you will surely die in your sins.^{John 8:24}

Yes, the burden rest on you; you alone must call upon the Lord Jesus as your personal Lord and Savior. No one else can make the decision for you. And remember, if you fail to call upon the Lord Jesus to save you, you have rejected the Lord Jesus and the only One that is able to rescue you from going to Hell. He is ready to receive you right now. Call upon Him now.

God promises you,

Then he called for a light, and sprang in, and came trembling, and fell down before Paul and Silas, [30]And brought them out, and said, Sirs, what must I do to be saved? [31]And they said, Believe on the Lord Jesus Christ, and thou shalt be saved, and thy house.   (Acts 16:29-31 KJV)

Footnotes:

1. *"Decision by default:"* when a person fails to act or make a decision within the proper set time, the decision is going into default. If anyone fails to make decisive decision to receive Christ, at death the person ends up in Hell by default. Making no decision for Christ is one's own undoing, and they go to Hell due to their sin and because they failed to call upon the Lord to be saved.

CHAPTER 3

There is no Turning Back

Memory verse

Then death and Hades were thrown into the lake of fire. This is the second death, the lake of fire. And if anyone's name was not found written in the book of life, he was thrown into the lake of fire.

(Rev. 20:14, 15)

Introduction

Friend, you need to know that if you do not make the decision to repent of your sins and call upon the Lord to save you right now, there is no turning back. You have to make a decision for Christ Jesus to be your personal Lord and Savior if you want be in Heaven.

Do you remember that if you do not make decision right now, you have actually made a decision which is **"no"** to Jesus Christ? Without your personal commitment and trust in Christ the Lord, you have said, **"No** to Jesus."[John 3:18, 36]

Jesus said plainly,

He that is not with me is against me; and he that *gathers* not with me *scatters* abroad. (Matt. 12:30 KJV)

The Sword, the Word of God, cuts two ways. This is a warning to both to the unbeliever as well as the believer. People had better pay attention here. First, if you have not made the commitment and trusted in Christ then you are standing against the Lord. Without your commitment and trust in the Lord Jesus, you have set yourself against Him. There is no so-called *neutral ground* or *sideline*. There is no sitting in bleachers or bench-seats with Jesus. You are either with Jesus or you stand against Him. If you are standing against the Lord Jesus, you will lose; you shall lose in Hell forever.

The same equally applies to the believer as to rewards or blessings in Christ. If you are not actively **worshipping** and **serving** the Lord through the local church, you are indeed of no value in furthering the Kingdom of God. If you profess faith in Christ but you are not actively serving through a church, you are **not** gathering! Friend, you are *scattering*. There is no sidelines or bench-seating with the Lord Jesus. If you are not active for Christ, you are a *dud* or *blank* or an *empty shell* and *useless* for the cause of Christ. You had better reexamine the legitimacy of your faith in Christ.

If you are a believer, be careful you do not say too quickly, "Amen." As I have said, the Sword of the Lord cuts through the person that only professes to be a believer and or those that imagine they can remain on the sidelines. That is, they can profess faith but they can remain *aloof, do nothing,* or *be passive* in the faith. Look at Jesus' statement again.

> "He who is not with Me is against Me; and **he who DOES NOT GATHER WITH ME SCATTERS.**" (Matt. 12:30)

Listen, you had better be putting your shoulder to the wheel and be laboring with other saints least you be found void of genuine saving faith in Christ. How many ways can I say it? There is no *neutral zone* with faith in Christ. Jesus said, '*he who does not gather with Me scatters.*' What are you doing for "**the gathering**" of the Kingdom of God? That is correct, "*What are you doing for the Kingdom of God?*" If you are doing nothing, well, I am here to tell you that Jesus warns all professing faith, '*he who does not gather with Me scatters.*' Well, my friend, are you one that is gathering, or are you one that is scattering?

If you are sitting like a "*knot on a log;*" you are of no value to Jesus. Since you are doing nothing; you better watch out. If you are doing nothing, you may be a person that only has a historical faith. Meaning maybe you have never been genuinely born from above [1] by the Spirit of God. There had better be a change in your life and in **worship** and **service**.

You cannot allege that you "love Jesus," but at the same time, you are doing nothing. If Jesus has not *permeated* or *absorbed* your life, He may not be the Lord of your life. If Christ is not the Lord of your life, He may not be the Redeemer of your life. Watch out!

Furthermore, you better not try to use the excuse, "Well, I have never been called." What? Listen carefully, Jesus **does** **not** give calls to serve Him. Friend, Jesus **GAVE A COMMAND.**

You might say to yourself, "Well, I love Jesus." Then, pay attention to Jesus' rebuke of the devil when our Lord said,

> And Jesus answered and said to him, "Get behind Me, Satan! For it is written, '**You shall <u>WORSHIP</u> the LORD** your God, and Him **only you shall <u>SERVE</u>.**'" (Luke 4:8 NKJ)

Maybe you think you know Jesus as your Lord and Savior. Oh, really? If you are not in church *worshipping* readily every Sunday and if you are not *serving* the Lord faithfully and regularly, you may be void of genuine saving faith in Christ. The Bible is very, very clear. Let us look at text from the NRS.

> For **the love of Christ urges** [compelling] **us on**, because we are convinced that one [Jesus Christ] has died for all [the believers]; therefore all [believers] have died [to self]. [15]And he [Christ] died for all [believers], so that those [believers] who live might live no longer for themselves, but [live] for him [Christ] who died and was raised for them [believers]. [16]From now on, therefore, we regard no one from a human point of view; even though we once knew Christ from a human point of view, we know him no longer in that way. [17]So if anyone is [truly] in Christ, there is a new creation [by regeneration the Spirit]: everything old has [now] passed away; see, everything has become new [creation]!
>
> (2 Cor. 5:14-17 NRS)

Listen my friend, has there been a change from above by the Holy Spirit since you professed faith in Christ? If there is **no basic change**, you had better reexamine the genuineness of being born from above. You cannot enter the Kingdom of God unless you have been born from above by the Holy Spirit. (It matters not what you claim to profess, unless you are born from above by the Spirit, you shall not see the Kingdom of God.) If you are born from above, do you desire worship and serve the Lord?

A. There is no reprieve

If you confess faith in Christ but that confession did not bring about a change in your life, I am warning you that you had better reexamine your confession of faith. Once you cross the threshold into eternity, there is no turning back; there is no reprieve.

Friend it is a terrifying thing to fall into the hands of the living God.[Heb. 10:31] It is great that you believe the historical facts of the Gospel.[1 Cor. 15:3, 4] Do believe in one God? Well, the demons also believe in one God, but demons also shutter. Do you shutter or tremble at the name of the Lord? Nonetheless, you still have to make a personal commitment and personally trust and receive Jesus as your Lord and Savior. If you made the personal commitment, is that commitment evidently *visible* and *measurable* in a new lifestyle in Christ? Believing the intellectual facts of the Gospel is the acknowledging the facts are true, but salvation comes only through a personal commitment and trust in Jesus as Lord and only Savior. Believing the facts is not necessarily evidence of regeneration. If one is truly saved, their life has been changed, and that change ought to be measurable for others to see in one's life.

The apostle Paul said of himself as given by the NRS,

> I know the one in whom **I have put my TRUST**[a], and I am sure that he is able to guard until that day what **I have entrusted** [*committed* KJV] **to him**. (1 Tim. 1:12b NRS)

> [a]Note: the GK word (*pisteuo*) "*believe*" is also translated "*trust.*" This is more than believing the facts that are true, there is implied a personal **trust** or even **commitment**.

The NRS has accurately captured the intended meaning here. Paul is not just believing the fact. Paul is trusting in Christ; he is not just believing the fact. Are you trusting in Jesus' sacrifice for sin, or are you just believing that Jesus died and arose?

Friend, please listen to me, there is no reprieve because your nature will not change in Hell. You will only be overwhelmed with bitterness and rage in Hell because you possess the same unregenerate nature. Do not say "No," as to question the genuineness of your commitment. Truly your anger will overtake you in Hell because if you were not born from above by the Holy Spirit, you did not receive the new nature that must come from above to enter the Kingdom of God.

No manmade religion can change you and give you a new nature; this is a new nature that is from above. If you took the time to read by footnote #1, then you know Jesus said very plainly as given by NRS.

> [5]Jesus answered, "Very truly, I tell you, no one can enter the kingdom of God without being born of water and Spirit. [6]**What is BORN OF THE FLESH IS FLESH**, and what is **BORN OF THE SPIRIT IS SPIRIT**. [7]Do not be astonished that I said to you, '**YOU MUST BE BORN FROM ABOVE.**' (John 3:5-7 NRS)

Just as there is the natural birth of being born into this world, there is also the supernatural birth that is **being born from above** into the Kingdom of God. And when you are genuinely born from above into the Kingdom of God, you receive a new nature that is given to you by the Holy Spirit. (Well, my friend, do you possess a new nature from above?)

When anyone is born from above by the Spirit of the living God, there comes with the nature from above a spiritual desire to worship and serve the Lord. If you do not have a hunger and trust for the Lord and His precious Word, then friend there is something wrong. You may only have historical faith but void of being born from above by the Holy Spirit.

Once you are truly born from above by the Spirit, you actually now possess two natures. You possess your natural nature given when born into this world. Then, when you are born from above, you receive a new nature, the indwelling of the Spirit of God. This is the new nature that comes from God. The apostle describes these two natures this way:

> *This* I say then, Walk in the Spirit, and ye shall not fulfil the lust of the flesh. [17]For the flesh *lusts*[b] against the Spirit, and the Spirit against the flesh: and these are contrary the one to the other: so that ye cannot do the things that ye would. [18]But if ye be led of the Spirit, ye are not under the law. (Gal. 5:16-18 KJV)

> [b]Note: the phrase here is the GK "*epithumeo kata*." The meaning is better translated, "longs after." Hence, "*its desire longs after*" or perhaps *passionately desires*.

So, there is the old nature that "longs after" the things of carnal life. Whereas, the new nature that is from above "longs after" the things of God. There is the struggle of the two natures within the genuine believer. Let us note the parallel between the old nature of the natural birth into this world and the new nature which is supernatural birth that is from above by the Spirit of God.

> [19] Now the works of the flesh are manifest, which are *these*; Adultery, fornication, uncleanness, lasciviousness [sensuality], [20] Idolatry, witchcraft, hatred, variance, emulations, wrath, strife, seditions, heresies [divisions], [21]Envyings [selfish rivalries, NET], murders, drunkenness, revellings, and such like: of the which I tell you before, as I have also told *you* in time past, that **they which do such things shall not inherit the kingdom of God.** [22]But the fruit of the Spirit is love, joy, peace, longsuffering, gentleness, goodness, faith, [23]Meekness, temperance [self-control]: against such there is no law. [24]And they **that are Christ's have crucified the flesh with the affections and lusts** [GK epithumeo, longing desire]. [25]If we live in the Spirit, let us also walk in the Spirit. [26]**Let us not be desirous of vain glory**, provoking one another, envying one another. (Gal. 5:19-26 KJV)

27

Do you see now my brother? If you have been genuinely born from above, then you should have **longing desire** to know and walk with the Lord Jesus. After all, is not Heaven a time to sing the praise of the Lord Jesus? If you do not have the desire to worship and serve the Lord now, what makes you think you will want to worship and serve the Lord in Heaven?

Salvation is not simply the acknowledging a fact of the truth of the Gospel. Salvation is even more than a regeneration. Salvation is a **new creation**, a transformation from above by the Spirit of God.

Paul did **not** see this change in some of the Corinthians. This why he questioned their genuineness of some of the people's saving faith in the church at Corinth. Note difference between the Latin Vulgate in ENG and KJV in 1 Cor. 3:4.

For while one saith, I am of Paul; and another, I *am* of Apollos; are ye not carnal? KJV	"For when one says, 'I follow Paul,' and another, 'I follow Apollos,' are you not being merely human?" LTE

The GK word in the KJV is *sarkikos*, refers to the **natural man**, the unregenerate, [1 Cor. 2:14], which is the same root word. The LV uses the word "**man**" (GK is *anthropos*). The original word in the GK was *sarkikos*, but Jerome change it to read "*man*" rather than *flesh* or *carnal*. I am going follow the BYZ text here.

Paul's rebuke is more than the rebuke *mere man*. Paul's rebuke is as though some Corinthians were still unregenerate and void of possessing the Holy Spirit. This is indeed why without evidence of regeneration by the Holy Spirit, Paul tells them (not asking them), "Examine yourselves, whether ye be in the faith," [2 Cor. 13:5 KJV]. Friend, if you do not have a longing for the Word of God or the desire to worship and serve the Lord Jesus, there is something wrong. You better reexamine your profession of faith in Christ.

B. The dye has been cast

If you are not willing to reexamine the genuineness of your faith in Christ, then *the dye has been cast* for you, and *there is no turning back*. You are being extremely stubborn and very, very foolish. Your resistance is not from the Spirit of God. You are allowing pride to control you, which is the natural man. Believing the Gospel is true and the only foundation for entering the Kingdom of God. We must be born from above by the Spirit of God. The Lord who gives us the *new nature* also gives us a *new view* on life. We are indeed a *new creation when we are genuinely saved*. The Holy Spirit gives us a *longing for the things of Heaven.*[Col. 3:1-4] Remember,

> But **the fruit of the Spirit** is love, joy, peace, forbearance, kindness, goodness, faithfulness, [23]gentleness and self-control. Against such things there is no law. [24]Those who belong to Christ Jesus **have crucified the flesh with its passions and desires.** [25]Since we live by the Spirit, let us keep in step [walk, be guided (NRS)] with the Spirit. [26]Let us not become conceited, provoking and envying each other.   (Gal. 5:22-26 NIV)

You had better be very careful; if you do not exhibit fruit of the Spirit, you may still be unregenerate and lost in sin. Again, if you do not have *a longing for the things of God*, you had better watch out. Friend, you had better reexamine the genuineness of your confession of faith. You need to reexamine the confession of your faith in Christ to determine whether you are in the faith.

John the Baptist was certainly saved, and John the Baptist was definitely *born from above* by the Spirit. It is very evident however that Nicodemus though he believed the Bible and came inquiring of the Lord Jesus, he was **not** yet born again into the Kingdom of God.

Nicodemus, like many Jews then and people today, imagine a person earns his way into God's Heaven. Even worse, man assumes he can set the standard or the basis for entering God's Heaven. My friend, how foolish is that when mankind can set the standard for Heaven and imagining that the God of Heaven will accept the standard man has set for himself? Do you see how foolish that would be?

Others imagine, "Well, if anyone obeys the Mosaic Law shall enter Heaven." Still others reason, "Well, if I obey the Ten Commandments, I will go to Heaven." The Word of God is very clear: *no one will be declared righteous or justified by the works of the Law.*

> "Knowing that a **man is not justified by the works of the law** but by **faith in Jesus Christ**, even we have believed in Christ Jesus, that we might be **justified by faith in Christ** and not by the works of the law; for **by the works of the law no flesh shall be justified.**"

> (Gal. 2:16 NKJ)

Sincerity will **not** get you into Heaven. Hell is paved with sincerity. God alone set the standard for Heaven, and His standard is trusting in Christ and having been born from above by the Spirit.
Friend, here is the kicker,

> [19]"For **I** through the law **died to the law that I might live to God**. [20]"I have been crucified with Christ; it is no longer I who live, but **Christ**

29

> lives in me; and the *life* which I now live in the flesh I live by faith in the Son of God, who loved me and gave Himself for me. ²¹"I do not set aside the grace of God; for if righteousness *comes* through the law, then Christ died in vain."
>
> (Gal. 2:19-21 NKJ)

Reformation, a change for good, will not get you into God's Heaven. You need regeneration through true genuine saving faith in the Lord Jesus, having been born from above by the Holy Spirit of God. As the apostle declares,

> For we also once were foolish ourselves, disobedient, deceived, enslaved to various lusts and pleasures, spending our life in malice and envy, hateful, hating one another. ⁴But when the kindness of God our Savior and *His* love for mankind [GK *philanthropia*] appeared, ⁵He saved us, not on the basis of deeds which we have done in righteousness, but according to His mercy, by the washing of regeneration and renewing by the Holy Spirit, ⁶whom He poured out upon us richly through Jesus Christ our Savior, ⁷so that being justified by His grace we would be made heirs according to *the* hope of eternal life. (Titus 3:3-7)

Well, my friend, have you received the "new birth?" Have you been born anew from above by the Holy Spirit? If you have been genuinely born from above, then you ought to possess a new nature. You ought to have a **longing or desire for the things of God**. If do not has such longing or desire for things of God, you had better reexamine the genuineness your faith in Christ.

Do you remember what Jesus said concerning some people that were claiming genuine faith in Him based upon their so-called *mighty works*, and they were even giving all the credit to the Lord? But He said to them,

> "Not everyone who says to me, 'Lord, Lord,' will enter the kingdom of heaven, **but only the one who does the will of my Father in heaven**. ²²On that day many will say to me, 'Lord, Lord, did we not prophesy in your name, and cast out demons in your name, and do many deeds of power in your name?' ²³Then I will declare to them, 'I NEVER KNEW YOU; go away from me, you evildoers.' (Matt. 7:21-23 NRS)

Jesus told us what is the will of the Father,

> For I have come down from heaven not to do my will but to do the will of him who sent me. ³⁹And **this is the will of him who sent me**, that **I shall lose none** of all those he has given me, but raise them up at the last day. ⁴⁰For my **Father's will is that everyone** who **looks to the Son** and **believes [*trusts*] in him shall have eternal life**, and I will raise them up at the last day." (John 6:38-40 NIV)

Some people only have a profession of faith. They may claim faith in Christ and even allege to work miracles in the Kingdom of God. The shocker comes when Jesus says to them, ""**I NEVER KNEW YOU.**""

Jesus does not say *I knew you once, but I do not know you any longer.* Jesus says, ""**I NEVER KNEW YOU.**"" Jesus is definitely declaring emphatically that He **NEVER KNEW THEM AT ANY TIME.**

Please *hear* and *heed* the warning: you cannot get into Heaven with a profession of faith. Friend, you better have been born from above by the Spirit of God. Otherwise, you will certainly perish in your sins.

Conclusion

My friend, listen to me, *there is no turning back; there is no retrieve.* Once you cross the threshold into eternity at death there is no turning back. Do not let your arrogance or the pride of the natural man within you to keep from reexamining whether you have been born from above.

Listen, sincerity paves the way into Hell. You need to be certain that you have passed from death into eternal life in Christ the Lord and Savior of your life, [John 5:24]. Let us each reexamine ourselves and be certain as the apostle Paul said,

> For I know the one in whom **I have put my trust**, and I am sure that he
> is able to guard until that day what I have entrusted to him.
>
> (2 Tim. 1:12b NRS)

Also, keep in mind, at death, *the dye has been cast*; it is too late to go back. Once we cross the threshold into eternity, it is too late. We cannot change anything once we die. Heaven is sure, and once we have placed our genuine trust in Christ and have been born from above by the Holy Spirit, we are indeed a citizen of Heaven today, right now.

However, if a person only has an intellectual profession of faith without having been born again through genuine saving faith in the risen Lord Jesus, they shall indeed perish forever in their sin. Friend, you can say at the Great White Throne Judgment: "Uh, I thought I had trusted in Christ Jesus as my Savior?" It will be too late.

Make certain you are in the faith. Remember, sincerity will only get you in to Hell. Make certain you have been born again through personally trusting and receiving Jesus as your Savior. You must be born from above by the Spirit through saving faith in the risen Lord Jesus Christ. Jesus said unless you believe "**I Am**" you will die in your sins.[John 8:24]

Footnotes:

1. "Born from above," John 3:3, 7, 31: the GK express is '*gennao anothen.*' *Genno* just means to be born. Ah, but the word *anothen* is used only 18 times in the NT, and 12 *anothen* is translated from *above* or meaning the *top*. For example, in [John 3:31], we read, "He that cometh from above [GK *anothen*] is above all: he that is of the earth is earthly, and *speaks* of the earth: he that *comes* from heaven is above all," John 3:31 KJV. There is no power by man or religion that can cause you to be born from above. Listen carefully, you can only born from above by the Holy Spirit through genuine saving faith in Jesus Christ as Lord and only Savior. This is why Jesus said,

   > Jesus answered, "Very truly, I tell you, no one can enter the kingdom of God without being born of water and Spirit. [6]What is born of the flesh is flesh, and what is born of the Spirit is spirit. [7]Do not be astonished that I said to you, 'You must be born from above.'   (John 3:5-7 NRS)

   There is then the natural birth being born of the flesh, and there is the supernatural birth by the Holy Spirit. Being born from above by the Holy Spirit is when we are made new creation in Christ.[2 Cor. 5:17] As Jesus said,

   > [6]What is born of the flesh is flesh, and what is born of the Spirit is spirit. [7]Do not be astonished that I said to you, 'You must be born from above.'   (John 3:6, 7 NRS)

CHAPTER 4

Let Your Loved-Ones Choose

Memory verse

"Sirs, what must I do to be saved?" [31] They said, "Believe in the Lord Jesus, and you will be saved, you and your household."

(Acts 16:30b, 31)

Introduction

The Lord our God has no grandchildren! There is no one in Heaven by proxy. If anyone wants to enter Heaven, they must personally call upon the Lord Jesus to save them, and then, he can be born from above by the blessed Holy Spirit. No one else can make that decision for you to be saved but yourself. This is the error of *electionists*. The *electionists* fail to recognize the human responsibility to personally make the commitment and place their trust in Christ's redemptive work on Calvary. If anyone does not personally call upon the Lord to save them, they will perish in their sin. Salvation is only through genuine personal commitment and trust in Jesus as Lord.

However, there is an except to the above rule. The unborn, infants, children, and the mentally ill are covered by the shed blood and death of Christ. This is because they are incapable of making a decision for Christ. Let me illustrate this point.

King David committed murder (killing Uriah, the husband of Bathsheba). David also committed adultery with Uriah's wife. The Lord took the life of his new born son, and upon the death of his son, the King said,

> But now he is dead, wherefore should I fast? can I bring him back again?
> I shall go to him, but he shall not return to me.   (2 Sam. 12:23 KJV)

At death of his son, David knew his son went to Heaven, and David also knew he would go to Heaven upon his death to be will his son.

I hope you do not believe the ecclesiastical lie that people wait in Hades until the resurrection of our Lord Jesus. The text in Luke 16:19-31 is **not a parable**; this a story of life. (While the story is likely a true event, I would be careful not to take everything in detail as literal.) Abraham's bosom is a metaphor for Heaven; it is not part of Sheol or Hades. Lazarus was not in Hades. At death, Lazarus was in Heaven with Abraham. (Jesus is clear that He saw Abraham in Heaven not in Hades[John 8:56]). The rich man, unbelievers, was in Hades. Friend, there is indeed a very great gulf between Heaven (Abraham's bosom) and Hades. So, the details are metaphorically given. This is because in Hades (or Sheol) and those in Paradise (or Heaven) do not know what is taking place elsewhere. I would be cautious or very careful not to press literalism to every aspect to the story of Lazarus and the rich man.

I warn you that if you insist on following the ecclesiastical fabrication of that lie (Abraham's bosom and Hades are just separate compartments) you will be held accountable. Remember James warning,

> My brethren, let not many of you become teachers, knowing that we
> shall receive a stricter judgment.   (James 3:1 NKJ)

Now as to the death, child, keep in mind that the children of a believing parent that child or children are sanctified. The children have been sanctified by grace because at least one parent is a believer.

> For the unbelieving husband is sanctified by the wife, and the
> unbelieving wife is sanctified by the husband: else were your children
> unclean; but now are they holy [GK *hagios*].   (1 Cor. 7:14 KJV)

Watch it here and do not read more than is implied here by the Scriptures. The words "*sanctified*" and "*holy*" are from the same root word. Meaning, those that have been ("*sanctified*" and "*holy*") have been "*set apart*" to hear the Gospel." The husband or wife who married a believing spouse is "*set apart*," and they have the opportunity more so to hear the Gospel and be saved. Paul is **not** saying the unbelieve spouse is somehow saved. The unbelieving spouse has a great opportunity to hear the Gospel and being saved.

The same is with the children in whom at least one parent is a genuine believer. The child is "*set apart*," and the children have more opportunity so to hear the Gospel and be saved. (Unsaved parents, the children have less opportunity to hear the Gospel.)

Also, any unborn, infant, child, or mentally ill is covered by the blood and death of Christ. If the child grows up but refuse to believe and receive Jesus as Lord and Savior, then, they shall indeed die in their sins and perish in Hell.

Paul's words to the Philippian jailer and those in his household must believe and receive the Gospel just like the jailor did. Paul said, 'Believe on the Lord Jesus Christ, and thou shalt be saved, and thy house.' Acts 16:31 KJV

Pay attention: Paul and Silas **do not** mean jailor's household would be saved because the jailor believed. Neither is there any inference for infant baptism. Water baptism occurred once the people believed the Gospel.

> At that hour of the night the jailer took them and [Paul and Salis] washed
> their wounds; then immediately he [the jailer] and all his household were
> baptized.   (Acts 16:33 NIV)

This is another concocted lie of ecclesiastical dogma. There is no reference or inference of infants' or children's water baptism. This is another form of eisegesis, the reading into the text Scripture that is **not implied**. Instead, let us practice exegesis, the *reading out of the text Scripture the intending meaning of the biblical author*.

A. Let your loved-ones have the opportunity

Unless you have made a definitive and decisive decision for Christ and you know for certain you have been born from above, do not leave your loved-ones dangling as to their salvation. Do not just share the Gospel. Listen, there is a need to plead with people to make a commitment and trust in the Lord Jesus. Time is running out. Do whatever you can to persuade them to come to Jesus Christ right now.

I had a person tell me, "Well, they have heard the Gospel." The inference implied is, "Well, it is on them." No! Friend, as a Christian, it is our responsibility to **persuade** our loved-ones to believe on the Lord Jesus. The problem with such reasoning is it fails to realize just maybe they **did not hear**! (That is right, maybe they did not hear the Gospel.)

Yes, they may have heard something of the Gospel, but it is also possible they did not really hear the Gospel clearly. First, do you know just hearing what another fully says is very complex and maybe the other person did not hear. Many things we tell others during a regular conversation are actually bypassed, ignored, or go over our head. (Often, we do not give our full attention in hearing others.) The full import of what is actually said is never completely heard or many times even misunderstood. So, communication is easily distorted or misunderstood even between spouses or even best of friends. As humans, we do not clearly hear much of the conversation. True! Even if language is the same and our friendship is very good and people know one another, communication can still be *very easily distorted* and even *misunderstood*.

Just look at marriages or family relationships. People cut one another off in their minds when listening to another person. They stop listening since they conclude that they got the gist of what was said before the other person completed their sentence. Even worse, some imagine they know what is in the other person's mind. This alone is sufficient to distort communication.

Communication easily breaks down between people more often than one may actually realize. Unfortunately, we are unable to properly communicate at times with one another. It is true my friend. This is part of the reason why marriages fracture, and there is a 50% divorce rate in the USA. (Even in the marriages that remain together, there is serious communication breakdown.) There is also the fracturing of communication between children and parents or grandparents. This is the reason, in part, communication breaks down in the work place. This is especially true between management and labor. In fact, even war can breakout between countries simply due to communication break downs. How sad is that?

Here is the heart of the problem: we assume (that's right, we assume that when speaking to others that the person <u>heard</u> and <u>fully</u> <u>understood</u>) our words. We do not even take the three strikes law into account: <u>the world</u>, <u>the flesh</u>, and <u>the devil's</u> interference. How detached is that?

Perhaps you might be thinking to yourself: yes, yes, I know all that-Friend, all the above is in the natural world. Many people are simply ill-informed concerning communication breakdown. Just as I alluded above in the spiritual world (supernatural realm), communication is many times worse. Communication is actually being hinted by the spiritual world. We struck out in the spiritual dimensions. Even far worse, the unregenerate has struck out in the natural man. It is very hard for the unsaved to actually fully hear the Gospel. Everything unfortunately get *"filtered"* through our depraved and corrupted minds. Friend, please listen, it very difficult for unsaved to hear the complete Gospel.

> The unbeliever [the natural man] does not receive the things of the Spirit of God, for they are foolishness to him. And he cannot understand them, because they are spiritually discerned.   (1 Cor. 2:14 NET)

Also, I cannot emphasize strong enough that the people have been mesmerized by the world's system. (Yes, there is a sense where the human hearts have been brain washed.) The Bible says that before we came to faith in Christ that we were "following the course of this world," [Eph. 2:1 ESV]. Friend, the world system is on collision course for Hell, and there is no way to stop this collision course since the world will not listen!

Finally, the Bible reveals this shocking reality,

> And even if our gospel is veiled [hid], it is veiled [hid] to those who are on the road to destruction [to Hell]. [4]The god[a] of this age[a] has **blinded the minds**[a] of those who don't have faith[a] so they couldn't see the light of the gospel [understand the Gospel] that reveals[a] Christ's glory. Christ is the image of God. (2 Cor. 4:3, 4 CEB)

> [a]Note: **five things** are happening here. 1). Satan is no god. He is finite created being, but he is blinding people from the Gospel. 2). The word is no *world*; the GK word is *aion*, *age*. 3). The *"world lies under the sway"* the evil one.[1 John 5:19 NKJ] He does not have world in his hands. 4). Satan hinders the Gospel, but he cannot keep anyone from being saved. 5). The Gospel needs to get through to people if they're going to be saved.

Satan works on the minds and emotions of unbelievers. He also works on the minds and emotions of believers to deceive. Let us remember that the Gospel is the power of God:

> For I am not ashamed of the gospel of Christ, for it is **the power of God to salvation** for everyone who believes, for the Jew first and also for the Greek. (Rom. 1:16 NKJ)

> For the preaching [GK logos, the Word] of the cross is to them that perish foolishness; but unto us which are saved it [the Word] **is the power of God**. (1 Cor. 1:8 KJV)

> For our gospel did not come to you in word only, but [the Gospel] also **in power and in the Holy Spirit** and with **full conviction**; just as you know what kind of men we proved to be among you for your sakes.
>
> (1 Thess. 1:5)

Finally, once more as given by the Amplified Bible,

> May the God of hope fill you with all joy and peace in believing [through the experience of your faith] that **by the power of the Holy Spirit** you will abound in hope *and* overflow with confidence in His promises.
>
> (Rom. 15:13 AMP)

Please note the statement once more: *Let your loved-ones have the opportunity*. That is, if you are indecisive and make no decision, do you want your loved-ones to miss the opportunity of Heaven? There is no middle of the road here. Listen, even if you are going make no decisions for Christ, please let your loved-ones have the opportunity to confess and receive eternal salvation in Christ Jesus as Lord and Savior. Let them have the opportunity to receive Christ through faith in Him and be made of citizen of Heaven right now, today. The question fits the other side of the equation. *Do you really want your loved-ones to follow* your example, especially if you make no decision for Jesus Christ? That is, do not assume they heard the Gospel. And certainly do not assume that they understood the Gospel. I have already explained the difficulty in communicate. If you cannot get it through your thick head, I am sorry. I guess I cannot get through to you that you are one that must seek to persuade your loved-ones to come to Christ right now. If you do not have the burden to persuade your loved-ones to come Christ right now while there is time, who then should carry this burden? Therefore, do not assume that because some are in church that they heard the Gospel and that they in fact actually understood the Gospel. There is the likelihood they did not fully understand the Gospel.

B. Ensure the family hears the Gospel invitation

First do not hand out a tract, and then, do **not assume** there was a Gospel invitation given and somehow, they understood. Listen Pastor, the unregenerate are *blind as a bat* to spiritual truths! I hope this point is abundantly clear from what was discussed above. Communication is very difficult in the natural realm. However, when it comes sharing the Gospel in the spiritual world or in the supernatural realm, communication and understanding is many times even more difficult due to the spiritual blindness, carnal minds, the world's influence, and demonic forces of war. Sadly, this is something very many Pastors and godly men fail to fully grasp or even realize.

First, the Gospel is **not** communicated by simply natural means. We cannot penetrate the darken minds of the unsaved through the natural senses. We are totally dependent upon the illuminating and penetrating power of the Holy Spirit going before us.

Unless the Spirit of God goes before us in presenting the Gospel, we are helpless. (This is why fervent and continual prayer is needed.) As Jesus said, "Without Me you can do nothing."[John 15:5] And again, *'the Spirit of God quickens or gives life, the flesh profits nothing,'* [John 6:63]. *The natural man receives not the things of God.*[1 Cor. 2:14] Satan is blinding people.[2 Cor. 4:3, 4] The Bible is clear concerning are warfare,

> For we wrestle not against flesh and blood, but against principalities, against powers, against the rulers of the darkness of this world, against spiritual wickedness in high *places.*   (Eph. 6:12 KJV)

The Bible is very clear how saving faith in Jesus Christ is to be communicated. Open the Bible and show the Gospel from the pages of God's Word. The Bible declares clearly and without any ambiguity,

> So then faith *comes* by hearing, and hearing by the word of God[b].
>
>   (Rom. 10:17 NKJ)

[b]Note: Some manuscripts read "the word of Christ."

So, the NET nicely translates it this way,

> Consequently faith comes from what is heard, and what is heard comes through the preached word of Christ (or *word of God*).
>
>   (Rom. 10:17 NET)

The Bible says this concerning the Jew, but his questions equally applies to everyone. Note Paul's questions, which are self-answering,

> How then will they call on him in whom they have not believed? And how are they to believe in him of whom they have never heard? And how are they to hear without someone preaching? (Rom. 10:14 ESV)

Of course, Israel heard the Gospel, but many Jews did not believe the Gospel. As Scriptures warns, many in Israel failed to heed God's Word; for it was of the Lord and His judgment upon Israel because their hearts were hardened against the Word of God.

The natural man is going to harden his heart and mind against the Word of God.[Psa. 95:8; Heb. 3:8, 15; 4:7] You and I cannot penetrate hardened heart and mind, but the Holy Spirit is able when He goes before us. Friend, we are totally dependent on the Holy Spirit in sharing the Gospel.

Nevertheless, saving faith comes from hearing clearly the Word of God.

> And we continually thank God because, when you received the *Word* of God [*from the apostles*] that you heard from us, you accepted it not as the word

39

of men, but as the true *Word* of God—the Word which is now at work in you who believe.   (1 Thess. 2:13 MSB)

For the *Word* of God is living and active, and sharper than any two-edged sword, even penetrating as far as the division of soul and spirit, of both joints and marrow, and able to judge the thoughts and intentions of the heart.   (Heb. 4:12)

James says,

In fulfillment of his own purpose he gave us birth [e.g., *causing us to be born*] by the *Word of Truth*, so that we would become a kind of first fruits of his creatures. (James 1:18 NRS)

Even the apostle Peter said as given by the Amplified Bible,

For you have been born again [that is, reborn from above—spiritually transformed, renewed, and set apart for His purpose] not of seed which is perishable but [from that which is] imperishable *and* immortal, *that is,* through the living and everlasting *Word* of God. (1 Peter 1:23 AMP)

Even giving people a Bible without explaining God's Word or giving a tract without an explanation of the Gospel, will come up short, people. Do you recall reading what the Ethiopian eunuch said to Philip? Philip asked, 'Do you understand what you are reading?' The man was well educated and he belonged to the official court of Candace, Queen of the Ethiopians.

So Philip ran up to it and heard the man reading Isaiah the prophet. He asked him, "**Do you understand what you're reading?**" [31]The man replied, "**How in the world can I, unless someone guides me?**" So he invited Philip to come up and sit with him. [32]Now the passage of scripture the man was reading was this: "He was led like a sheep to slaughter, and like a lamb before its shearer is silent, so he did not open his mouth. [33]In humiliation justice was taken from him. Who can describe his posterity? For his life was taken away from the earth." [34]Then the eunuch said to Philip, "Please tell me, who is the prophet saying this about– himself or someone else?" [35]So Philip started speaking, and beginning with this scripture proclaimed the good news about Jesus to him. [36]Now as they were going along the road, they came to some water, and the eunuch said, "Look, there is water! What is to stop me from being baptized?" [37c] [38]So he ordered the chariot to stop, and both Philip and the eunuch went down into the water, and Philip baptized him. [39]Now when they came up out of the water, the Spirit of the Lord snatched Philip away, and the eunuch did not see him *anymore*, but went on his way rejoicing.

(Acts 8:30-39 NET)

' Note: Verse 37 **is** in the **BYZ, Coptic, Latin Vulgate**, but unfortunately, verse 37 is not found in **many older GK texts**. What's omitted? Then Philip said, "If you believe with all your heart, you may." And he answered and said, "I believe that Jesus Christ is the Son of God."[Acts 8:37 NKJ] It is likely not part of the original GK text.

The Ethiopian was well educated and wealthy because he had a copy of Isaiah (perhaps more Scripture.) Philip ask the man,

"Do you understand what you are reading?" And he said, "How can I, unless someone guides me?"   (Acts 8:30, 31 NKJ)

So, what is the over point? Faith, if it is going to be realized and believed. We must follow up on people:

a). Saving faith must be given with a clear presentation. We need to present the Gospel personally to people or through preaching and hearing the Gospel. (This must include one on one presentation of the Gospel whenever possible.)

b). Presenting the Gospel is clearer when people not only hear the Gospel but when the Gospel is shown; the Bible is opened and showing them the Scriptures.

c). We need to ask the person directly, "Would you like to receive Jesus as your personal Lord and Savior right now?"

d). We need to lead the person through the process of confessing and receiving Jesus as their personal Lord and Savior, [Rom. 10:9-13].

e). **Avoid telling them that they are saved** if they confess Christ. Instead, **show the promise of God** [Rom. 10:13]. If they truly trust in Christ, He will save them.

Conclusion

Well, my friend, "Do you want your loved-ones follow your example?" You loved-ones have the right to hear the Gospel. So, please help them to hear the Gospel clearly and completely. This means hearing the Gospel and giving them the opportunity to repent and receive Jesus Christ as Lord and Savior.

If you are a believer, please do not assume your loved-ones heard the Gospel fully and completely. **Satan wants you assume they heard and understood.** Please do not be so callous and do nothing and think to yourselves, "It is up to them to decide." It is likely that they **do not know** what the Gospel truly is. So, how in the world are your loved ones going to be able to make a decision for Christ?

Moreover, I have shown communication breaks down among the best family members or friends in the natural world. How much more difficult communication in spiritual realm? Friend, we must do our best to help the unsaved hear the Gospel, and yes, someone help explain and persuade people to come to Jesus before it is too late.

We owe it to our loved-ones and friends to clearly hear and understand the Gospel. Let us not assume that they understand the Gospel. Please, our loved-ones must be given the opportunity to say "Yes" or "No," but if they said no, someone needs to persuade them with a godly rebuttal from the Word of God. You cannot reach the unregenerate through natural reasoning. In all likelihood, they do not know what Gospel is, and it is for certain they do not know how to make decision for Christ.

The biggest mistakes in giving the Gospel are: 1). Christians wrongly assume people **understand the Gospel**. 2). Many people do not know even **how to receive the Gospel**. 3). Most do not want the Gospel because the **Gospel is an offense to them**. Ah, but once they come to Jesus, they are glad they did. Hallelujah!

Let us help our loved-ones and friends hear and understand the God.

Part Two

The Lord and Heaven are beyond description

CHAPTER 5

The Door into Eternal Love and Forgiveness

Memory verse

"He will wipe away every tear from their eyes; and there will no longer be *any* death; there will no longer be *any* mourning, or crying, or pain; the first things have passed away." (Rev. 21:4)

Introduction

Nowadays there are *charlatans, evil workers, and false prophets*, and *fake healers* claiming to have gone to Heaven and come back again. They claim to be able to describe and tell in detail the full event. These are people similar to what Jude says in his epistle,

It is these worldly people, devoid of the Spirit, who are causing divisions. (Jude 1:19 NRS)

Many of these people are unfortunately self-deluded and duped by their overactive carnal minds. They may be sincere, but they have given themselves over to a carnal and overly imaginary depraved mind. Such people have not made any trips to Heaven and returned to tell about it.

Others may have been influenced by demons, since demons are capable of working people's carnal mind and emotions. Demons approach the mind as though they are angel of light from God.[2 Cor. 11:13-15]

Yet, there are others that may have been given illusions by demonic forces. Such illusions are deadly because it is possible they saw or heard things that

45

appeared as though they were from God. We know that in the temptation of our Lord Jesus by Satan that the kingdoms of this world were shown to Him. However, it appears this was likely illusion but seemed very real.

Still others are liars and fabricators and void of any godly truth. They have no fear of God, unless of course they are simple-minded and empty of any rational reasoning. If they are simple-minded, they are simple, and are what The Bible calls a fool. But these are not ignorant people. This are cunning or shrewd operators fleecing people of their hard-earned money.

Still, there were two apostles that did experience entering Heaven and being in the presence of God and returned to this world. As we already noted, the apostle Paul and the apostle John were translated into the heavenly realm. However, neither apostle gave any description concerning Heaven, and this is because they were not permitted to reveal such revelation. In the apostle Paul's heavenly experience, he says,

> [2]I know a person in Christ who fourteen years ago was **caught up to the third heaven**[a]—whether in the body or out of the body I do not know; God knows. [3]And I know that such a person—whether in the body or out of the body I do not know; God knows— [4]was **caught up into Paradise** and **heard things that are <u>NOT</u> to be told**, that <u>NO</u> <u>MORTAL</u> <u>IS</u> <u>PERMITTED</u> <u>TO</u> <u>REPEAT</u>. [5]On behalf of such a one I will boast, but on my own behalf I will not boast, except of my weaknesses. [6]But if I wish to boast, I will not be a fool, for I will be speaking the truth. But I refrain from it, so that no one may think better of me than what is seen in me or heard from me, [7]even considering the exceptional character of the revelations. Therefore, to keep me from being too elated, a thorn was given me in the flesh, a messenger of Satan to torment me, to keep me from being too elated. [8]Three times I appealed to the Lord about this [*thorn in the flesh*], that it would leave me, [9]but he said to me, "My grace is sufficient for you, for [*My*] power is made perfect in weakness." So, I will boast all the more gladly of my weaknesses, so that the power of Christ may dwell in me. [10]Therefore I am content with weaknesses, insults, hardships, persecutions, and calamities for the sake of Christ; for whenever I am weak, then I am strong.   (2 Cor. 12:2-10 NRS)

[a]Note: The sky is the first heaven(s). The stars are possibly the second heaven(s). The third may be the actual abode of God, Heaven itself.

Paul uses the same word Jesus used to refer to Heaven, "*Paradise.*"[Luke 23:43; 2 Cor. 12:4; Rev. 2:7] My friend, if the apostle Paul was **NOT** permitted to give any detail of Heaven, I am convinced **"no other mortal is permitted to repeat**."[2 Cor. 12:4]

Similarly, the apostle John tells us,

> I was in the Spirit on the Lord's day, and I heard behind me a loud voice like *the sound* of a trumpet, saying, "Write in a book what you see, and send *it* to the seven churches:" (Rev. 1:10, 11)

> [17]When **I saw Him** [*the risen Christ*], **I FELL AT HIS FEET LIKE A DEAD MAN**. And He [*Jesus Christ*] placed His right hand on me, saying, "Do not be afraid; I am the first and the last, [18]and the living One; and I was dead, and behold, I am alive forevermore, and I have the keys of death and of Hades. [19]Therefore write the things which you have seen, and the things which are, and the things which will take place after these things." (Rev. 1:17, 18)

Whether John was in a vision or like Paul caught up to the third Heaven, it is not clear. One thing for certain, John was *petrified* in the presence of the risen and glorified Lord Jesus Christ.[Rev. 1:17] I suspect the apostle John was given a heavenly vision with the divine revelation. However, John was not permitted to write some things concerning Heaven. Yet, he was instructed to write some events. In one vision, he was not permitted to discuss the seven thunders.[Rev. 10:3, 4] This seems to suggest that the various sets of "sevens" were not the same issues. John's revelation was limited. It is likely that the set of *"seven peals of thunder"* [NAS, Rev. 10:3, 4] have not been fulfilled" as many seem to assume. What John saw and was allowed to reveal in his writings was very restricted. He did not even know for certain somethings that he was seeing many times.

Therefore, let us be very careful, and let us not go beyond what is written in God's Word. Caution is very necessary because many times we do not know what we have actually experienced in the natural world. So then, how much more difficult is it when it comes to knowing what he/she has experienced in the supernatural world and with things of God? Nevertheless, Heaven is very real, and Hell for that matter is very real as well. Yet, the Lord has revealed some things concerning Heaven in His precious Word.

A. Love and eternal peace that is incomprehensible

The psalmist said,

> The LORD will fulfill his purpose for me; **your steadfast love, O LORD, endures forever**. Do not forsake the work of your hands.

47

(Psa. 138:8 ESV)

Another great psalm as given by the NRS,

> O give thanks to the LORD, for he is good, for **his steadfast love endures forever**. (Psa. 136:1 NRS)

As to the love of Christ the Lord, the apostle says,

> As it is written: "For your sake we face death all day long; we are considered as sheep to be slaughtered." [37]No, in all these things **WE ARE MORE THAN CONQUERORS** through him who loved us. [38]For I am convinced that **neither death nor life, neither angels nor demons, neither the present nor the future, nor any powers,** [39]**neither height nor depth, nor anything else in all creation**, will be able to separate us from the love of God that is in Christ Jesus our Lord. (Rom. 8:36-39 NIV)

Friend, there is nothing in all creation able to separate us from the love of God in Christ Jesus our Lord. Our Lord created the universe.[John 1:1-3, 10; Col. 1:16,17; Heb.1:2] The cults that lie and distort the Gospel allege that we are like a dog at death. The cults teach that at death, all life is non-existent. There is no life existing after death until God gives life to their bodies once again. (This is according to the lying cults.) The apostle says "neither death nor life" is able to separates us from the love of God. This is the apostle Paul that can say even if he faces death,

> For to me to live *is* Christ, and **to die *is* gain**. [22]But if I live in the flesh, this *is* the fruit of my *labor*: yet what I shall choose I wot not. [23]For I am in a strait betwixt two, having a **desire to depart, and to be with Christ; which is far better**: (Phil. 1:21-23 KJV)

What does it mean when we read after the thousand-year reign of Christ in the new Earth and new Heaven and even a new Jerusalem,

> And I saw a new heaven and a new earth: for the first heaven and the first earth were passed away; and there was no more sea. [2]And I John saw the holy city, new Jerusalem, coming down from God out of heaven, prepared as a bride adorned for her husband. [3] And I heard a great voice out of heaven saying, Behold, the tabernacle of God *is* with men, and he will dwell with them, and they shall be his people, and God himself shall be with them, *and be* their God. [4] **And God shall wipe away all tears from their eyes**; and there shall be no more death, **neither sorrow, nor crying, neither** shall there be **any more pain**: for

the former things are passed away. [5] And he that sat upon the throne said, Behold, I make all things new. And he said unto me, Write: for these words are true and faithful.   (Rev. 21:1-5 KJV)

Friend, this a scene in Heaven and perhaps a glimpse into the new universe. God's Word declares, 'God shall wipe away all tears from their eyes.' This is indeed is the tenderness and love and mercy that God shall surely give to His redeemed.

Many mock the above scene as nothing more than a *metaphor*, an *allegory*, or just *symbolism* not literally true. My friend, this comes from **God who cannot lie**.[Titus 1:2] This is more than *always telling the truth* as one had translated the above verse. The Lord our God is so holy and righteous that "In hope of eternal life, which God, that **cannot lie, promised before the world began** [GK *pro chronos aionios*, lit. "*before time of the ages began*"].["][Titus 1:2 KJV]

This is a promise that God made before the ages were unfolded. This is the tender love of God being revealed in Heaven: '*God shall wipe away all tears from their eyes.*'

Why the tears in Heaven? Listen friend, some people who only had a profession of faith in Christ were never saved. Other were following "a god" of their own manufacturing. Yes, their faith was not in Jesus Christ of the Bible. Still others, their god was "mother nature;" they followed the lie of evolution. Yes, they drank of the poison of atheism. Well, it is for sure that there are no atheists in Hell; they know the Bible is true since their abode is now in Hell.

There is everlasting peace as well

Besides the love that is everlasting to the redeemed now and in eternity, there is also a "peace" that is our now and continues throughout eternity. Hallelujah! This is a peace that the wealthiest person in the world is unable to buy. This is an eternal peace now in this life and in the life throughout eternity that no psychiatrist or psychologist can provide.

Best of all, we are given a true Friend that will never leave us or forsake us.[Heb. 13:5] (Friend I am talking about **a friend right now**, in the here and now as well as **a friend throughout eternity**.) This means that the true believer shall never be left alone. Glory to God! It is true my friend. Even death cannot separate us from our Friend. This Friend is **Yehoshua** in HEB, but those know Him call him **JESUS**. Hallelujah!

As the angel Gabriel declared to the virgin Mary and as he revealed to her concerning Elizabeth a relative of hers.

> And behold, your relative Elizabeth in her old age has also conceived a son, and this is the sixth month with her who was called barren. **For nothing will be impossible with God.**" (Luke 1:36, 37 ESV)

Jesus said,

> Peace I leave with you, my peace I give unto you: not as the world giveth, give I unto you. Let not your heart be troubled, neither let it be afraid. (John 14:27 KJV)

For those who walk with the world, or those engulfed with self, or even worse those entangled by the devil, they have no peace. Nevertheless, peace is indeed free to all that truly receive Jesus as Lord and Savior and walk in His will. Those who walk with the world and their love for the world set themselves in hostility to God.[1John 2:15-17]

We are not to walk with the world.[Cor. 3:1-4] Let us not carry out filthiness of the flesh,[2 Cor. 7:1]. By the grace of God, let us put on the whole armor of God to do battle with the evil force.[Eph. 6:10-18] Let us walk with Jesus who alone gives us this peace. He will prove.[Phi. 4:19] Jesus told his apostles, which has spiritual application to the believers today,

> [25]"For this reason I say to you, do not be worried about your life, *as to* what you will eat or what you will drink; nor for your body, *as to* what you will put on. Is not life more than food, and the body more than clothing? [26]Look at the birds of the air, that they do not sow, nor reap nor gather into barns, and *yet* your heavenly Father feeds them. Are you not worth [*valuable*] much more than they? [27]And who of you by being worried can add a single cubit to his life span? [28]And why are you worried about clothing? Observe how the lilies of the field grow; they do not toil nor do they spin, [29]yet I say to you that not even Solomon in all his glory clothed himself like one of these. [30]But if God so clothes the grass of the field, which is *alive* today and tomorrow is thrown into the furnace, *will He* not much more *clothe* you? You of little faith! [31]Do not worry then, saying, 'What will we eat?' or 'What will we drink?' or 'What will we wear for clothing?' [32]For all these things the Gentiles eagerly seek; for your heavenly Father knows that you need all these things. [33]**BUT SEEK <u>FIRST</u> <u>HIS</u> <u>KINGDOM</u> AND <u>HIS</u> <u>RIGHTEOUSNESS</u>, and all these things will be added to you**. [34]So do not worry about tomorrow; for tomorrow will worry about itself. Each day has enough trouble of its own." (Matt. 6:25-34 LSV)

There are liberals, cults, and even hyper-dispensationalists that deny the above Scripture and blessings apply to the saints today. But King David says,

> I was young and now I am old, yet I have never seen the righteous forsaken or their children begging bread. (Psa. 37:25 NIV)

The application is not the evil doctrine "Name and Claim it." Such teachers are liars and wicked and Hell awaits them. They are void of any truth, and they have given themselves over to a deceiving lie.

Friend, if you will genuinely place your full commitment and sole trust in the risen and glorified Lord Jesus Christ and walk in His will and Word (the Bible), He will indeed care and watch over you. I know, like King David, I have been there and am doing it right now.

Ah, but what comes with this friendship with **JESUS** is the peace that the world cannot give. Listen, as I have already said, this is peace right now. This is a friendship that does not just last a lifetime. This is Friend and friendship that is yours right now, and the friendship will continue throughout your life even into eternity. Get this eternal life while you can. This friendship is free to all will come unto Jesus. He gives this wonderful promise right now,

> Come to me, all you who are weary and burdened, and I will give you rest. [29]Take my yoke on you and learn from me, because I am gentle and humble in heart, and you will find rest for your souls. [30]For my yoke is easy to bear, and my load is not hard to carry." (Matt. 11:28-30 NET)

B. Forgiveness and goodness rest on you forever

My friend, there is good news for you that regardless of how wicked and evil you have been, Christ will forgive you of all your sins and clean up from the inside out. You see, religion is manmade. Religion tells you that *you must first change your life. You must clean your life up on your own. It is up to you to meet their standard.* Then, *just maybe, their god will receive you.*

Ah, but there is a wonderful song that declares what the Lord will do for you when you repent of your sin and genuinely commit your life to Him as you place your complete trust in Jesus and walk in His will.

Surely Goodness and Mercy[1]

1. A pilgrim was I and a-wandering,
In the cold night of sin I did roam,
When Jesus the kind Shepherd found me,
And now I am on my way home.

Chorus
Surely goodness and mercy shall follow me
all the days, all the days of my life
Surely goodness and mercy shall follow me
all the days, all the days of my life.

2. He restoreth my soul when I'm weary,
He giveth me strength day by day,
He leads me beside the still waters,
He guards me each step of the way.

3. When I walk through the dark lonesome valley,
My Savior will walk with me there;
And safely His great hand will lead me
To the mansions He's gone to prepare.

The truth is that none of us are able to clean up our life sufficiently to be acceptable before the Lord our God, the only God. But here is the Good News: Jesus died in your place for sin. That is right, the Lord Jesus Christ paid the full price for our sins on the cross. He shed His blood and dying on the cross. He was buried and arose on the third day. Hallelujah, He is coming to receive all those that have put their full commitment and trust in Him as Lord and only Savior.

First, when you genuinely receive Jesus as your Lord and Savior, He will surely forgive you of all you sins. He will make you His child. Yes, the Lord will make you a citizen of Heaven right now, today. Yes again, it is true, He will make you a citizen today, right now. When we genuinely receive and trust the Lord Jesus, His gives this sure promise,

> But **our citizenship is in heaven** [*immediately transferred into Heaven*].
> And we eagerly await a Savior from there, the Lord Jesus Christ, [21]who,
> by the power that enables him to bring everything under his control,
> will transform our lowly bodies so that they will be like his glorious
> body. (Phil. 3:20, 21 NIV)

Friend, do you see it now? God's Word does not say our citizenship is going to be in Heaven. His Word says, "our citizenship **is** [now] in Heaven!" Once more, yes, we are made citizens of Heaven the moment we genuinely commit our life to Jesus Christ as Lord and Savior. But first you must call upon Him to save you and forgive you of your sins. You must make a **full**

commitment and **solely trust** in shed blood and death in your place for sin on the cross.

Immediately, your sins are gone forever, as He has cleansed and made you completely righteous through genuine saving faith in the Lord Jesus. He put the Holy Spirit within you, making you holy and righteous as His servant forever.

Listen please, He is the very best Friend you will ever have right now in this life. He shall not only be your best Friend in this life, but He will also even be your very best Friend in the life to come in Heaven.

If you have made the commitment and trusted in Christ Lord- follow these steps to guide you along the way:

1. **Talk to the Lord** Jesus frequently throughout the day or night **in prayer** and always **giving thanks**.

2. Get a contemporary translation, if possible, like the NAS or NIV. If you only have a **KJV, that is very fine**. Start reading through the Gospel of John at least three times. Then begin with Paul's epistles including Hebrews (Romans through Hebrews, reading the letters three times.) Then begin to read the OT and NT. (Alternate in reading the OT and NT.)

3. Pray as you **look** for a sound and **good Bible Church** to worship with and that preaches all the Bible and believes in water baptism by immersion. (Water baptism does not save you, but it is an act of obedience in our faith.)

4. Faithfully **worship and serve the Lord** regularly. You ought to give 10 percent to the Lord since tithing is a universal principle in the Bible. Make certain, as much as possible, that all your loved ones trust and receive Jesus as Lord and Savior. Encourage your loved-ones to follow you in a sound Bible church. (This is because many, many churches and denominations have forsaken the Bible and Jesus' mandates.)

Besides **forgiveness** now and for eternity in Christ, there is **goodness** that will follow you all the days of your life on earth and yes, continue throughout eternity in Heaven. There is no greater Scripture with such wonderful promise which King David wrote. This is again another psalm by King David who wrote:

> The LORD *is* my shepherd; I shall not want. ²He *makes* me to lie down
> in green pastures: he *leads* me beside the still waters. ³He *restores* my

soul: he *leads* me in the paths of righteousness for his name's sake.
⁴Yea, though I walk through the valley of the shadow of death, I will
fear no evil: for thou *art* with me; thy rod and thy staff they comfort me.
⁵Thou *prepared* a table before me in the presence of mine enemies: thou
anointed my head with oil; my cup [*is*] *running* over. ⁶**Surely goodness
and mercy shall follow me all the days of my life: and I will dwell in
the house of the LORD forever**.   (Ps. 23:1-6 KJV)

David committed some serious sins, but he found forgiveness and goodness in the Lord His God. Friend, I am telling you I know this is true because
forgiveness and goodness have followed all the days of my life. Hallelujah, I
too will dwell in the house of the Lord forever in Heaven forever, amen.

Surrender your life to the Lord Jesus, and walk in faith and obedience in
His Word. I can promise you that goodness shall follow you all the days of
your life. Not only that, but you shall indeed dwell in the house of the Lord
forever in Heaven! Know this also, the Bible says that all who live godly in
Christ will suffer persecution in Christ Jesus.[2 Tim. 3:12] Jesus will never forsake
or leave those whom He has redeemed.[Heb. 13:5] He will walk with you through
every trial. The Bible gives us this sure promise from God who cannot lie.

Therefore let anyone who thinks that he stands take heed lest he fall.
No temptation has overtaken you that is not common to man. **God is
faithful**, and he will not let you be tempted beyond your ability, but
with the temptation he will also provide the way of escape, that you may
be able to endure it.   (1 Cor. 10:12, 13 ESV)

There is blessing waiting for all those that truly know Jesus as Lord and
Savor and walk in faith and obedience to His Word. Here is another blessed
promise:

Now may the God of peace, who brought up from the dead the great
Shepherd of the sheep through the blood of the eternal covenant, *that is,*
Jesus our Lord, equip you in every good thing to do His will, working
in us that which is pleasing in His sight, through Jesus Christ, to whom
be the glory forever and ever. Amen.   (Heb. 13:20, 21)

There is a blessing awaits all those who genuinely commit their life to
Jesus as Lord and Savior and walk with His Word seeking to do His will. There
is no greater Shepherd than Jesus. There is no greater Friend who can give you
complete forgiveness of all your sins and provide goodness all the days of your
life even in the midst of the trials of life.

If you want your life to change right now and change for the better, then Jesus is ready and willing to make you a new creation.

> Therefore, if anyone is in Christ, the new creation has come: The old has gone, the new is here! (2 Cor. 5:17 NIV)

Conclusion

This is the door into eternal love and forgiveness right now. No one can take away what God has given you in Christ. It is yours free when you genuinely commit and place your complete trust in Jesus as Lord and Savior. But friend you must act right now today. The Bible is very clear when God's Word tells us, "Behold, now is the acceptable time, and behold, now is the day of salvation."[2 Cor. 6:2 ABPE]

Love and eternal peace that is incomprehensible is yours for the taking. This a love that can begin right now, and Jesus' love will continue into eternity in Heaven with the Lord our God. This is a love of God that neither life or death can separate from His infinite incomprehensible love.

There is peace that Jesus gives us, and no one can take it away.[John 14:27] The richest person in the world cannot buy this peace, but it is free through genuine saving faith in Jesus Christ as your personal Lord and Savior.

Forgiveness and goodness rest on you forever, which continues now and throughout eternity in Heaven in Christ. Regardless your sins, Jesus will take away your sin. As the psalmist says,

> As far as the east is from the west, so far does he remove our sins[b] from us. (Psa. 103:12 GNT)

> [b]Note: the HEB word is *pesha*. The word actually means *transgression* or implying an act *rebellion*.

As to goodness, my friend, several chapters could be easily written without exhausting the great Psalm 23. Remember the song "Surely Goodness and Mercy" describes that *"Surely goodness and mercy shall follow me all the days of my life, and I shall dwell in the house of the Lord forever,"* and yes in Heaven.

Yes, it is true: Jesus is the greatest Friend you will have now in this life, and the life to come in Heaven. But listen, you must genuinely place your trust in Him right now. Have you put your trust in Him as Lord and Savior? Do it right now; He is waiting to receive you. Most of all, **walk in complete faith** and **obedience to Jesus** and **His Word** because He is the greatest Friend you will ever have right now and throughout eternity.

Footnotes:

1. "Surely Goodness and Mercy" originally sung by Diana Leagh Matthews. The hymn, written in 1958 and based on Psalm 23, was the collaboration of two well-known gospel music writers, John W. Peterson and Alfred B. Smith.

CHAPTER 6

The Door into
the Presence of God

Memory verse

Therefore, brethren, since we have confidence to enter the holy place by the blood of Jesus, [20]by a new and living way which He <u>inaugurated</u>[a] for us through the veil, that is, His flesh, [21]and since *we have* a great priest over the house of God, [22]let us draw near with a sincere heart in full assurance of faith, having our hearts sprinkled *clean* from an evil conscience and our bodies washed with pure water. [23]Let us hold fast the confession of our hope without wavering, for He who promised is faithful.   (Heb. 10:19-23)

[a]Note: "*inaugurated*" [NAS] is the GK "<u>*egkanizo*</u>;" [KJV] "*consecrated*" and as to "*renew*," "*dedicated*," or perhaps "*opened*." <u>*Inaugurated*</u> is preferred.

Introduction

Do you know that there are *hyper-dispensationalists* that allege the monumental epistle of Hebrew is not for the church? Such expositors, no doubt, are very committed to such interpretation; but friend, sorry, I beg to differ with them!

Still, while the New Covenant (has been inaugurated), the fullness of that covenant will not be realized until the Lord reestablishes His covenant with Israel.[Jer. 31:31ff] (Upon the reestablishing Israel as covenant people, I would agree.) Paul, the chief scribe of the NT, said,

57

> Who also made us sufficient as ministers of the new covenant [b], not of
> the letter but of the Spirit; for the letter kills, but the Spirit gives life.
>
> (2 Cor. 3:6 NKJ)

> [b]Note: true the GK read "**a new covenant**." There is no definite article
> "the." This is avoiding the issue: *we are servants of the New Covenant*.
> Yet, the fullness of that covenant cannot fully be realized without Israel
> in covenant relationship as the Lord fully and surely will fulfill.[Jer. 31:31ff]

We must realize that the Hebrews writer fully saying, he is declaring that
as believers in Christ we have access into the very presence of God in Heaven
through the blood and death of the Lord. Not just the blood but also Jesus'
death on Calvary. The shed blood and death of Christ Jesus are inseparable
in out redemption. (Some only emphasize Christ's death, but His shed blood
is equally important in redemption.) The blood and death are woven together
as one single act: Christ Jesus' sacrifice for sin on the cross. As Hebrews says
once again,

> Since, then, we have a great high priest who has passed through
> the heavens [*into Heaven itself*], Jesus, the Son of God, let us hold fast to
> our confession. [15]For we do not have a high priest who is unable to
> sympathize with our weaknesses, but we have one who in every respect
> has been tested as we are, yet without sin. [16]Let us therefore **approach
> the throne of grace with boldness**, so that we may receive mercy and
> find grace to help in time of need.   (Heb. 4:14-16 NRS)

Under the Old Covenant through Mosaic Law, the high priest only enters
the holy of holies but only on Yom Kippur (the Day of Atonement) and not
without blood. Hebrews writer explains,

> But the high priest [under the old covenant] alone goes into the inner one [the holy of
> holies] once a year, not without [sacrificial] blood that he offers for himself and
> for the sins of the people.   (Heb. 9:7)

If the priest enters the holy of holies unclean under the Old Covenant,
the high priest will be struck dead. (This is why some say that a rope was
tied on his foot. So, if God struck him dead, those outside the holy of holies
could pull him out safely without danger to their lives.) But now, through
sacrifice of Jesus Christ on the cross, we have access into the presence of
God. The Old Covenant was only a copy of the real Holy of Holies in Heaven.
Friend, we enter now into actual Holy of Holies in Heaven itself by the blood

and death of Jesus Christ on the cross. Can someone say with me hallelujah and amen!

A. Into the presence of God, it is indescribable

Wonders of wonders: there is no one in this world able to describe the wonderful mystery and the greatness and marvels of the Lord Jesus' redemption on the cross. Weymouth NT right implies correctly,

> Because it is through Him [Jesus Christ] that Jews and Gentiles alike have access [access into the very presence of God] through one Spirit to the Father.
>
> (Eph. 2:18 WNT)

Friend, this is access into the presence of God in Heaven, and it is ours right now in Christ, today. Our access is now when we are saved and pray through Jesus Christ as our Lord and Savior. Even before we pray, the Lord already know your heart and mind. This is the very reason Christianity is not a religion. Friend, genuine saving faith in Jesus Christ is a living and vibrant relationship with the eternal God. This access is ours when we truly know Jesus as Lord and Savior. Praise the Lord!

You or I do not have direct and immediate access to such people as the President of the United States of America and perhaps other high officials in the world. However, we have access to the King of kings, the Lord of lords, and to the only Sovereign One over the entire universe. This is at any time and for anything.

> This is the confidence which we have before Him, that, if we **ASK ANYTHING ACCORDING TO HIS WILL, HE HEARS US**. And if we know that He hears us *in* whatever we ask, we know that we have the requests which we have asked from Him. (1 John 5:14, 15)

Why should we ask according to the will of God? This is because the Lord knows what is best. Friend, His will is always, I mean always, better than our will. The Lord can see around the corner. Listen, we can't see around the corner. We cannot see what is coming ahead, but praise the Lord, the Lord sees what is coming ahead. This means the Lord is ready and able to deal with all situations on our behalf. We do not know if our request is good or really bad for us. Ah, but the Lord knows what is best for us.

This access into Heaven to God's Presence is perpetual

Jude gives us a glimpse of the wonderful perpetual access into Heaven. No human merits access into the presence of God. Sin separates us from God.

Ah, but Jude declares the boldness we have in Christ Jesus as he gives an awesome doxology that ought to cause us stand up and shout out loud with extreme joy,

> Now to Him who is able to keep you from stumbling, and to make you stand in the presence of His glory blameless with great [*exuberance*] joy, to the only God our Savior, **through Jesus Christ our Lord**ᶜ, *be* glory, majesty, dominion and authority, before all time and now and forever. Amen. (Jude 1:24, 25)

> ᶜNote: the phrase "*through Jesus Christ our Lord*" is not found in the BYZ text, but it is a tremendously important phrase. The phrase is indeed important in the doctrine of Christology in the NT.

How can we who know ourselves well and are honest as to our real character go into the very presence of the Lord our God who is forever and ever holy and righteous? It is more certain no mortal in his unregenerate nature is worthy to stand in God's presence because He is indeed infinite in holiness and righteousness.

Listen, even the Seraph angels were created holy and righteous and they are without sin. Still, the seraphim fly in the presence of God: cover their faces with two wings, and with two wings cover their feet, and with two wings fly. The Seraphs cry out loud, 'Holy, holy, holy *is* the LORD of hosts; The whole earth *is* full of His glory!'[Isa. 6:3 NKJ]

All of us as humankind before the Lord are wretched, undone, and very wicked. All mankind regardless of their religion can do nothing but stand condemned and silent before the Lord. Ah, but glory to God, Christ the Lord died in place of the genuine believer. Every person who genuinely commits their life to Jesus as Lord and Savior, God imputes[2 Cor. 5:21; Phi. 3:9] to them. They are sealed with the Holy Spirit unto the day of redemption.[Eph. 4:30]

The Bible is very clear,

> And be found in him [Christ], not having a righteousness of my own, that which is of the law, but that which is through faith in Christ, the righteousness which is from God by faith [in Christ]. (Phi. 3:9 WEB)

We are made righteous **not** on the basis of faith. Get it right, we are made righteous on the basis of **our being in Christ the Lord**.
The apostle Paul said to the Corinthians,

> God made him who had no sin to be sin for us, so that in him we might become the righteousness of God. (2 Cor. 5:21 NIV)

60

But ye are of him in Christ *Jesus*[d], who of God is made *unto us wisdom* and *righteousness*, and sanctification, and redemption,

(1 Cor. 1:30 GNV)

[d]Note: The words in italics have not been changed; only the spelling is updated.

Once again, the apostle says,

[9]Have you not known that the unrighteous will not inherit the Kingdom of God? Do not be led astray; neither whoremongers, nor idolaters, nor adulterers, nor effeminate, nor sodomites, [10]nor thieves, nor covetous, nor drunkards, nor revilers, nor extortioners, will inherit the Kingdom of God. [11]And certain of you were these! **But you were washed**, but **you were sanctified**, but **you were declared righteous**,[e] in the Name of the Lord Jesus, and in the Spirit of our God. (1 Cor. 6:9-11 LSV)

[e]Note: the word righteous is the same word for justified, *dikaioo*. Righteous is preferred because we have been imputed the righteous of Christ.

Hence, as Jude declares we will enter Heaven faultless.[Jude 1:24, 25] We shall be received with great joy because the Lord has removed all our sins. Yes, praise the Lord, He has imputed to us the righteousness of Christ for all those who truly trust Jesus as Lord and only Savior.

Friend, there is no hanging our heads down as we enter Heaven at death. As Jude declares,

— to present *you* faultless before the presence of his glory with exceeding [*exuberance*] joy- (Jude 1:24b KJV)

However, it will be the most terrifying day for the unbeliever without Christ as Lord and Savior.

Then I saw a great white throne and Him who sat on it, from whose face the earth and the heaven fled away. And there was found no place for them. [12]And I saw the dead, small and great, standing before God, and books were opened. And another book was opened, which is *the Book* of Life. And the dead were judged according to their works, by the things which were written in the books. [13]The sea gave up the dead who were in it, and Death and Hades delivered up the dead who were in them. And they were judged, each one according to his works. [14]Then

> Death and Hades were cast into the lake of fire. This is the second death. [15]And anyone not found written in the Book of Life was cast into the lake of fire. (Rev. 20:11-15 NKJ)

The unbeliever will be petrified and speechless as he/she stands before an infinitely holy and righteous God. The Bible says, "there was found no place for them."[Rev. 20:11b] This is because the Lake of Fire awaits them. Hebrews gives this dreadful warning,

> Anyone who rejected the law of Moses died without mercy on the testimony of two or three witnesses. [29]How much more severely do you think someone deserves to be punished who has trampled the Son of God underfoot, who has treated as an unholy thing the blood of the covenant that sanctified them, and who has insulted the Spirit of grace? [30]For we know him who said, "It is mine to avenge; I will repay," and again, "The Lord will judge his people." [31]It is a dreadful thing to fall into the hands of the living God. (Heb. 10:28-31 NIV)

B. Into the presence of God, wonderfully true

Listen, Jesus said to the unbelieving Sadducees that God is the God of the living and not of the dead.

> 'I am the God of Abraham, the God of Isaac, and the God of Jacob'? He is not the God of the dead but [He is the God] of the living!"
>
> (Matt. 22:32 NET)

The saints that die are very much alive in Heaven,

> When He opened the fifth seal, I saw under the altar the souls of those who had been slain for the word of God and for the testimony which they held. [10]And they cried with a loud voice, saying, "How long, O Lord, holy and true, until You judge and avenge our blood on those who dwell on the earth?" [11]Then a white robe was given to each of them; and it was said to them that they should rest a little while longer, until both *the number of* their fellow servants and their brethren, who would be killed as they *were*, was completed. (Rev. 6:9-11 NKJ)

The saints, the true believers in Christ, are alive waiting to receive the resurrection and transformation of our bodies.[Rom. 8:22f; Phi. 3:20, 21] Yes, the saints in their souls join the Holy Spirit by inviting people to come to Jesus as Lord and Savior while there is still time to receive Christ as their Redeemer,

And the Spirit and **the bride** say[f], Come. And let him that heareth say, Come. And let him that is athirst come. And whosoever will, let him take the water of life freely.   (Rev. 22:17 KJV)

[f]Note: the word "say" in GK is plural, _lego_. _Lego_ is plural because not only is the Holy Spirit beckoning and appealing to people to come Jesus right now. Also, the bride, the saints in Heaven, are saying "come."

The plea is from the saints which are saying, "Heaven is wonderful." That is right, the bride, which are the saints that died, and their bodies have yet to be raised from the dead. Nevertheless, Heaven is wonderful, and the saints in Heaven are saying, "Come on up and join us; it is truly wonderful."

Friend, you cannot make it to Heaven with good works. Jesus has paid the full price, and it is free by His grace. The Bible says,

For the wages of sin is death, but **the free gift of God is eternal life in Christ Jesus our Lord**.   (Rom. 6:23)

The Bible is clear,

For by grace you have been saved through faith, and that not of yourselves; _it is_ the gift of God, [9]not of works, lest anyone should boast. [10]For we are His workmanship, created in Christ Jesus for good works, which God prepared beforehand that we should walk in them.

(Eph. 2:8-10 NKJ)

Friend, those who have gone to Heaven are telling us that Heaven is real and it indeed a wonderful place. However, to enter Heaven the Bible says we must be borne from above by the Holy Spirit through genuine saving faith Christ the Lord. As Jesus told Nicodemus (a believer in the Bible but not yet redeemed),

Jesus answered him, "Very truly, I tell you, no one can see the kingdom of God without being born from above." [4]Nicodemus said to him, "How can anyone be born after having grown old? Can one enter a second time into the mother's womb and be born?" [5]Jesus answered, "Very truly, I tell you, no one can enter the kingdom of God without being born of water and Spirit. [6]What is born of the flesh is flesh, and what is born of the Spirit is spirit. [7]Do not be astonished that I said to you, 'You must be born from above.'   (John 3:3-7 NRS)

Conclusion

Heaven is *the Door into the Presence of God*. You will never make it to Heaven by good works. This is because all our works are filthy stench, and we cannot wash away our sins by so-called good works or by water baptism. As NET gives the literal translation,

> We are all like one who is unclean, all our so-called **righteous acts are like a menstrual rag** in your sight [*O Lord*]. We all wither like a leaf; our sins carry us away like the wind.　　　　　　(Isa. 64:6 NET)

Come now while the door into the Presence of the Lord is available, but you have to come right now. The risen Lord Jesus is offering the door into His Heaven and into His Presence,

> And He said to me, "It is done! I am the Alpha and the Omega, the Beginning and the End. I will give of the fountain of the water of life freely to him who thirsts."　　　　　　(Rev. 21:6 NKJ)

CHAPTER 7

The Door to Reunion and Joy

Memory verse

But while he was still a long way off, his father saw him and felt compassion *for him*, and ran and embraced him and kissed him.

(Luke 15:17)

Introduction

If you have a very close friend (I mean a friend closer than a brother or sister), then, parting brings many tears and emptiness of joy. There is sorrow and sometimes pain when close friends depart. The Bible speak of close friendship when Scripture says,

Some friends don't help [a], but a true friend is closer than your own family.[a]　　　　　　　　　　　　　　　　(Proverbs 18:24 CEV)

[a]Note: the HEB word is <u>ach</u>, literally "*brother*." The HEB expression is difficult. See the NKJ and NET below for comparison.

A man *who has* friends must himself be friendly, But there is a friend *who* sticks closer than a brother.　　　　　　(Prov. 18:24 NKJ)

A person who has friends may be harmed by them, but there is a friend who sticks closer than a brother.　　　　　　(Prov. 18:24 NET)

David and Jonathan were such close friends, seemingly closer than brothers. The wicked and depraved minds look at such friendship as a homosexual relationship. A wicked person perverts the truth of a godly friendship, and they lie. At the death of King Saul and his son Jonathan, King David said,

Then David chanted this lament over Saul and his son Jonathan. [18](He gave instructions that the people of Judah should be taught "The Bow." Indeed, it is written down in the Book of Yashar.) [19]The beauty of Israel lies slain on your high places! How the mighty have fallen! [20]Don't report it in Gath, don't spread the news in the streets of Ashkelon, or the daughters of the Philistines will rejoice, the daughters of the uncircumcised will celebrate! [21]O mountains of Gilboa, may there be no dew or rain on you, nor fields of grain offerings! For it was there that the shield of warriors was defiled; the shield of Saul lies neglected without oil. [22]From the blood of the slain, from the fat of warriors, the bow of Jonathan was not turned away. The sword of Saul never returned empty. [23]Saul and Jonathan were greatly loved during their lives, and not even in their deaths were they separated. They were swifter than eagles, stronger than lions. [24]O daughters of Israel, weep over Saul, who clothed you in scarlet as well as jewelry, who put gold jewelry on your clothes. [25]How the warriors have fallen in the midst of battle! Jonathan lies slain on your high places! [26]I grieve over you, my brother Jonathan! You were very dear to me. Your love was more special to me than the love of women. [27]How the warriors have fallen! The weapons of war are destroyed!   (2 Sam. 1:17-27 NET)

The wicked and perverted minds misinterpret the tribute and lament of just men like King Saul and Jonathan. The NET does justice to David's lament of Jonathan as translated,

> I grieve over you, my brother Jonathan! You were very dear to me. Your love was more special to me than the love of women.

(2 Sam. 1:26 NET)

Like the Song of Solomon, the natural man (the wicked and the depraved minds) are consumed with lust and sensual appetite as he distorts God's Word. Watch out, my brother, and be careful that you are not driven by carnal and wicked mind of the unregenerate when reading God's Word. The Lord is a holy and righteous God, but may He pay back double anyone that perverts the Word of God like carnal trash and wicked lies.

A. Hallelujah, many of our loved-ones will be there

The world today is so overcome with wickedness that there seems to be little shame. This is even among many so-called Christians. People are not shocked at the evil that plagues our society. Even our little ones (innocent children) are being scorched with wickedness through TV, videos, music, internet, and even in public school where they're taught about sex at a very young age. Friend, I am here to tell there is little shame felt today.

Yet, in the midst of this present sorrow and grief, Heaven is now our permanent and real residence for all those in Christ. Yes, Heaven awaits us with the reunion of our loved-ones. We are no longer citizens of this world. We now belong to Christ the Lord, and so, we are *sojourners and strangers* in this world.[1 Peter 2:11] Like I said above, this is a reunion even with a friend that sticks closer than a brother.

Yes, even those forgotten and long gone are loved-ones we never knew. "Frank, loved-ones we never knew?" Yes, don't you know that the children that many of us lost due their early and untimely death. Yes, some may have been miscarriages, or they died as a child. We never really got to know them. My friend, there is a reunion of loved-ones we never got to really know in this world. However, there is a wonderful reunion waiting for us in Heaven.

It is okay if you smile in your skepticism and cynicism, but like King David said, it shall be wonderfully realized in Heaven. Remember, at the death of David's son by Bathsheba, he said,

> But now he has died; why should I fast? Can I bring him back again? I
> am going to him, but he will not return to me." (2 Sam. 12:23)

Children you have had you either forgot that you had or children you did not realize you had due to miscarriage will be in Heaven. This is a reunion not just for us who depart at death into Heaven, but friend, this is joy for the children who never knew their parents. Regrettably, some parents will not be in Heaven; this is because they were never truly born from above by the Holy Spirit through faith Christ the Lord. But parents that were genuinely saved in Christ, this will be a mutual happy and joyous reunion. Of course, the children that died young will not be little ones in Heaven. They shall be fully mature. Also, we will no longer know one another as parent or loved-ones, but we shall indeed know one another. What a wonderful and glorious day with a reunion in Heaven.

Some may say, "But I how shall we know our children?" The Lord will make that clearly known to us. Friend, there will be no doubt. The apostle Paul says,

> [8]Love never fails. But where there are prophecies, they will cease; where
> there are tongues, they will be stilled; where there is [prophetic] knowledge,
> it will pass away. [9]For we know in part and we prophesy in part, [10]but
> when completeness comes, what is in part disappears. [11]When I was a

child, I talked like a child, I thought like a child, I reasoned like a child. When I became a man *[fully mature as a man]*, I put the ways of childhood behind me. [12]For now we see only a reflection as in a mirror; then **we shall see face to face**. Now I know in part; **then I shall know fully, even as I am fully known**.

(1 Cor. 13:8-12 NIV)

We shall know one another "even as I am fully known."[1 Cor. 13:12 NIV] Job (the oldest book in the Bible), the man Job in the midst of what he must have felt as the sense of pending death, remarked,

[25]But as for me, I know that my Redeemer lives. In the end, he will stand upon the earth. [26]After my skin is destroyed, then I will see God in my flesh, [27]whom I, even I, will see on my side. My eyes will see, and not as a stranger. "My heart is consumed within me." (Job 19:25-27 WEB)

The apostle John even says,

[1]See how great a love the Father has given us, that we would be called children of God; and *in fact,* we are.[c] For this reason, the world does not know us: because it did not know Him. [2]Beloved, now we are children of God, and it has not appeared as yet what we will be. We know that when He appears, we will be like Him, because we will see Him just as He is. [3]And everyone who has this hope *set* on Him purifies himself, just as He is pure.

(1 John 3:1-3)

[c]Note: John is saying that all who have genuinely trust in Christ Jesus as Lord and Savior are children.

John continues noting the differences between those only professing faith in Christ and those who truly possess genuine saving faith in Christ.

This is how we know who the children of God are and who the children of the devil[d] are: Anyone who does not do what is right is not God's child, nor is anyone who does not love their brother and sister. (1 John 3:10 NIV)

[d]Note: John does **not** mean that the devil has offspring. John is using metaphorical language, and the unregenerate follow the evil one.

Neither does our Lord mean that the devil has offspring [John 8:44] nor the apostle John means that the devil has children. The meaning implied is that the unregenerate possess only the old nature.[Gal. 5:16-18] Hence, the unregenerate live like the devil, they do evil things rather than living a godly life doing things that please the Lord.

B. It is true, there is inexpressible joy

There is a reciprocal joy that is sometimes easily overlooked. There is indeed a great blessing being with the Savior in Heaven in our souls whom we shall see when our eyes close at death and our bodies are in the grave. Don't you know, my brother, Jesus tells the unbelieving Pharisees that Abraham saw Christ the Lord in Heaven. Here is the dialogue:

⁵¹Verily, verily, I say unto you, If a man keep my saying, **he shall never see death**.

⁵²Then said the Jews unto him, Now we know that thou hast a devil [GK *daimonion, demon*]. Abraham is dead, and the prophets; and thou sayest, If a man keep my saying, he shall never taste of death.

⁵³Art thou greater than our father Abraham, which is dead? and the prophets are dead: *who make* thou thyself?

⁵⁴Jesus answered, If I *honor* myself, my *honor* is nothing: it is my Father that honors me; of whom ye say, that he is your God: ⁵⁵Yet *you* have not known him; but I know him: and if I should say, I know him not, I shall be a liar like unto you: but I know him, and keep his saying.

⁵⁶Your father **Abraham rejoiced to see my day**: and **he saw *it*, and was glad**.

⁵⁷Then said the Jews unto him, Thou art not yet fifty years old, and **hast thou seen Abraham**?

⁵⁸Jesus said unto them, Verily, verily, I say unto you, **Before Abraham was, I AM**. [See Exodus 3:13-15]

⁵⁹Then took they up stones to cast at him: but Jesus hid himself, and went out of the temple, going through the midst of them, and so passed by.   (John 8:51-59 KJV)

Just as Abraham saw Christ the Lord after death in Heaven, in the same way, friend, those that are genuinely redeemed in the Lord shall see our Redeemer as Job also says ᴶᵒᵇ ¹⁹:²⁵ᶠᶠ.

This is not just our joy being in Heaven. Friend, look, there is joy expressed by the Father, the Son, and Holy Spirit when we reach Heaven being in Christ. Note Jude's doxology once more, there is jubilance by God,

Now unto him that is able to keep you from falling, and to **present *you* faultless before the presence of his glory WITH EXCEEDING**

JOY, [25][*to the only God our Savior, through Jesus Christ our Lord*]ᵉ
To the only wise God our *Savior, be* glory and majesty, dominion and
power, both now and ever. Amen.   (Jude 1:24-25 KJV)

ᵉNote: the phrase in italics is omitted in the BYZ text (KJV), but the
phrase is genuine and belongs in the text. (See the author's book on
Jude.)

My friend, do you know the story of "the Parable of the Prodigal Son," in
Luke 15:11-32? The prodigal son was given his inheritance. The young man
squandered his inheritance, and he became destitute and famished in a foreign
land.

[17]"But when he [*they young man*] came to himself, he said, 'How many of my
father's hired servants have more than enough bread, but I perish here
with hunger! [18]I will arise and go to my father, and I will say to him,
"Father, I have sinned against heaven and before you. [19]I am no longer
worthy to be called your son. Treat me as one of your hired servants.'"
[20]And he arose and came to his father. But while he was still a long way
off, his father saw him and felt compassion, and ran and embraced him
and kissed him. [21]And the son said to him, 'Father, I have sinned against
heaven and before you. I am no longer worthy to be called your son.'
[22]But the father said to his servants, 'Bring quickly the best robe, and put
it on him, and put a ring on his hand, and shoes on his feet. [23]And bring
the fattened calf and kill it, and let us eat and celebrate. [24]For this my son
was dead, and is alive again; he was lost, and is found.' And they began
to celebrate.   (Luke 15:17-24 ESV)

My brother, we are wicked sinners (every one of us). We are prodigal sons
and daughters of the living God. Just as the father ran to greet his prodigal son,
so, the heavenly Father will greet us with great joy.
This is why I say that there is *reciprocal joy*. There is as Jesus said,

Just so, I tell you, there **WILL BE MORE JOY IN HEAVEN** over **one
sinner who repents** than over ninety-nine righteous persons who need
no repentance.   (Luke 15:7 ESV)

If there is joy by the Lord greeting His redeemed as they enter Heaven,
how much more will our joy be when we are kissed by the Savior? As the
apostle Peter says,

[3]Blessed be the God and Father of our Lord Jesus Christ, who according
to **His great mercy** has caused us to be born again [GK *anagennao, born anew, e.g.*

regeneration] to a living hope through the resurrection of Jesus Christ from the dead, [4]to *obtain* an inheritance *which is* imperishable, undefiled, and will not fade away, **RESERVED IN HEAVEN for you**, [5]who are **protected by the power of God** through faith for a salvation ready to be revealed in *the* last time. [6]**In this you greatly rejoice**, even though now for a little while, if necessary, you have been distressed by various trials, [7]so that the proof of **your faith**, *being* **more PRECIOUS THAN GOLD** which perishes though tested by fire, may be found to result in praise, glory, and honor at the revelation of Jesus Christ; [8]and though you have not seen Him, you love Him, and though you do not see Him now, but believe in Him, **you greatly rejoice with JOY INEXPRESSIBLE AND FULL OF GLORY**, [9]obtaining as the outcome of your faith, the salvation of your souls.   (1 Peter 1:3-9)

My friend, what a reunion this will be. As Jim Hill who wrote the hymn below,

"What A Day That Will Be." [1]

1. What a day that will be When my Jesus I shall see And I look upon his face The one who saved me by his grace When he takes me by the hand And leads me through the Promised Land What a day, glorious day that will be (in the second person)

2. There'll be no sorrows there No more burdens to bear No more sickness and no more pain No more parting over there But forever I will be With the one who died for me What a day, glorious day that will be

3. What a day that will be When my Jesus I shall see When I look upon his face the One who saved me by his grace (but when he) When he takes me by the hand (takes me by the hand) And leads me through the Promised Land What a day, glorious day that will be

4. Oh, what a day that will be When my Jesus I shall see When I look upon his face The one who saved me by his grace (but when he takes me by the hand) And leads me through the Promised Land What a day, glorious day that will be

Yes, amen, it is true; there will be inexpressible joy by the Lord. And friend, what a joy when we see Jesus the one who saved us by His grace, what a day of rejoicing that shall be for you and me.

Conclusion

Oh yes, my friend, *this is the Door to Reunion and Joy*. At death, sorrow will be turned into joy. This is because many of our loved-ones will be there. Our loved-ones in Christ will be there, and it shall be a wonderful and glorious union in Heaven. Are you looking forward to seeing loved-ones? Some will be a reunion you know, but are the loved-ones you never knew ones you shall be eager to meet in Heaven?

Sadly, there were others that refused to make a commitment and personal trust in Jesus as Lord and Savior; they will not be there. Others only had a profession faith without truly being born from above by the Spirit of God. Sadly, they will not be there. These are people simply lost and in sin without a Redeemer, and they shall not be there. Plead with your loved-ones while there is still time; plead that they will repent and truly receive Jesus as their personal Lord and Savior.

There is inexpressible joy for the reunion. My wife had at least one and maybe two miscarries. I am looking forward to meeting these loved-ones I never knew. I had a young sister who died very young and before I was born. I am looking forward to meeting her. Praise the Lord!

Do you know of a child or children dying very young? Well, if you are genuinely trusting in Christ, you will get to meet them. There is going to be inexpressible joy; what a day that will be.

Footnotes:

1.   "What A Day That Will Be," written by Jim Hill in 1955.

CHAPTER 8

The Door to Rewards and Blessings

Memory verse

"And whoever gives one of these little ones just a cup of cold *water* to drink in the name of a disciple, truly I say to you, he shall by no means lose his reward." (Matt. 10:42)

Introduction

Just being in Heaven rather than Hell is sufficient enough reward for any redeemed in Christ. The saints in Christ do not labor for the Lord our God for rewards. We serve Him because He first loved us, and now we love the Lord. As John says,

We love Him [a] because He first loved us. (1 John 4:19 NKJ)

[a]Note: while the pronoun "*Him*" is omitted by many MSS, the BYZ GK text reflect the natural flow: "We love **Him** because He first loved us." Without the pronoun "**Him**," the sentence is incomplete.

The Lord our God initiated or open the flood gate of His infinite and marvelous love to the entire world. This is plainly declared to us by one of greatest verses in the Bible,

"For **God so loved the world**, that **He gave His only begotten Son**, that **whoever believes in Him shall not perish**, but [*he shall*] **have eternal life**." (John 3:16)

Please keep in mind the Lord is *making available* or *extending* His marvelous love to each person in the world. Yet, the world **is not** a recipient of the Lord of God. The love of God is being made available in Christ to each person in the world. As the apostle John continues by saying,

> *He* that *believes*[b] in him [*Christ Jesus the Lord*], is not condemned: but *he* that *believes* not, is condemned already, because he *has* not *believed* in the Name of that *only* begotten *Son* of God.　　　　(John 3:18 GNV)

> [b]Note: no words have been changed in the GNV; only the spelling has been updated. Word in brackets "[ ]" are for clarity but not in the GK texts.

Then, John concludes chapter three with this startling revelation:

> "He who believes in the Son has everlasting life; and he who does not believe[c] the Son shall not see life, but the wrath of God abides on him."　　　　(John 3:36 NKJ)

> [c]Note: the words "not believe" is one word the GK *apeitheo*. *Apeitheo* means to *disobey*, but it is also used to mean *refuse heed* the Gospel. E.g., "But the unbelieving [*apeitheo, refuse to heed the Gospel*]. E.g., "Jews stirred up the Gentiles, and made their minds evil affected against the brethren."[Acts 14:2 KJV]

Unfortunately, there are some who have a profession of faith, but they, unfortunately, do nothing for the Lord. Why do they do nothing? Some only have a profession faith or just an intellectual acknowledgement of truth of the Gospel, and sadly, they remain unregenerate and lost in sin forever. There are others, though they have been truly saved for many years, they have done little or nothing for the Lord. They rarely attend church faithfully. They rarely give faithfully to the church, and they give little or nothing to missions. Perhaps Jude has some of these people in mind when he says,

> Save others, snatching them out of the fire; and on some have mercy with fear, hating even the garment polluted by the flesh.　　(Jude 1:23)

However, be careful yourself because Peter says,

> For it is time for judgment to begin with God's household; and if it begins with us, what will the outcome be for those who do not obey [*apeitheo, disbelief*][d] the gospel of God? [18]And, "If it is hard [*with difficulty*] for the righteous to be saved, what will become of the ungodly and the sinner?"

[19]So then, those who suffer according to God's will should commit themselves to their faithful Creator and continue to do good.

(1 Peter 4:17-19 NIV)

[d]Note: see "[c]" above on the GK word *apeitheo*, disbelief, disobey; hence, to *refuse to heed the Gospel* or *reject the Gospel*.

A. It is true; it's all by the grace of God

Heaven's entrance is solely by faith through grace of the Lord Jesus. Heaven is attained by the infinite mercy and grace of the Lord Jesus through trusting Him. There is no other entrance or way into Heaven but Jesus and Him alone. (Our Lord not only created Hell. He created Heaven, and it is His Heaven.) Only manmade religions boast before "a god" that he has manufactured in his futile and depraved mind. However, there will be no boasting in Heaven. Those in Heaven have been saved by His grace and grace alone.

For **by grace are ye saved through faith**; and that not of yourselves: *it is* **THE GIFT OF GOD**: [9] **Not of works**, lest any man should boast. [10]For we are his workmanship, **created in Christ Jesus unto good works**, which God hath before ordained that we should walk in them. (Eph. 2:8-10 KJV)

Some of the saints withdraw or deny their faith in Christ due to persuasion and suffering for their faith in Christ. Hebrews, however, encourages us to be steadfast in the faith.

But recall the former days when, after you were enlightened, you endured a hard struggle with sufferings, [33]sometimes being publicly **exposed to reproach and affliction**, and sometimes being **partners with those so treated**. [34]For you had **compassion on those in prison**, and you **joyfully accepted the plundering of your property**, since you knew that you yourselves had a better possession and an abiding one [e.g., *possession in Heaven*]. [35]Therefore do not throw away your confidence, which has **a GREAT REWARD**. [36]For you have **need of endurance** [*persevere*]**, so** that when you have done the will of God you **MAY RECEIVE WHAT IS PROMISED** [e.g., *reward*]. [37]For, "Yet a little while, and the COMING ONE will come and will not delay; [38]but my righteous one shall live by faith, and if he shrinks back, my soul has no pleasure in him." [39]**But we are not of those who shrink back and are destroyed, but of those who HAVE FAITH and PRESERVE THEIR SOULS.** (Heb. 10:32-39 ESV)

Jesus left this world and ascended to Heaven to prepare a place for every one that truly has trusted in Him as Lord and Savior.

> "Do not let your heart be troubled; believe in God, believe also in Me. ²In My Father's house are many dwelling places; if it were not so, I would have told you; for I go to prepare a place for you. ³If I go and prepare a place for you, I will come again and receive you to Myself, that where I am, *there* you may be also. ⁴And you know the way where I am going." ⁵Thomas said to Him, "Lord, we do not know where You are going, how do we know the way?" ⁶Jesus said to him, "I am the way, and the truth, and the life; no one comes to the Father but through Me."
>
> (John 14:1-6)

What kind of Heaven would it be if it were on based on works? People could be boasting in what they did to attain Heaven. Listen my friend, there shall be no boasting since we know we deserve to be in Hell. Yes, we are saved by the Lord's infinite mercy and grace.

> For we also once were foolish, disobedient, deceived, serving divers [*every kind of*] lusts and pleasures, living in malice and envy, hateful, hating one another. ⁴ But when the kindness of God our *Savior*, and **HIS LOVE TOWARD MAN**, appeared, ⁵**not by works** *done* in righteousness, which we did ourselves, but according to **his mercy he saved us**, through the **washing of regeneration** and **renewing of the Holy Spirit**, ⁶which he poured out upon us richly, through Jesus Christ our *Savior*; ⁷ that, **being justified by his grace**, we might be **made heirs according to the hope of eternal life**. (Titus 3:3-7 ASV)

The Bible is very clear that we are saved by grace through faith alone through Jesus Christ our Lord.

> But if it is by grace, it is no longer on the basis of works, otherwise grace is no longer grace. (Rom. 11:6)

Our salvation is through the Lord Jesus' **propitiatory** [1] sacrifice for sin. In sacrifice of Himself on the cross (dying in our place for sin), the Lord Jesus *placated the wrath* of God on behalf of every believer.

> ²¹But now the righteousness of God has been manifested apart from the law, although the Law and the Prophets bear witness to it— ²²the righteousness of God through faith in Jesus Christ for all who believe. For there is no distinction: ²³for all have sinned and fall short of the glory of God, ²⁴and are justified [*made righteousness*]ª by **his grace as a gift**, through the redemption that is in Christ Jesus, ²⁵whom God put forward

as a **propitiation** by his blood, to be received by faith. This was to show God's righteousness, because in his divine forbearance he had passed over former sins. [26]It was to show his righteousness at the present time, so that he might be just and the justifier of the one who has faith in Jesus. [27]Then what becomes of our boasting? It is excluded. By what kind of law? By a law of works? No, but by the law of faith. [28]For we hold that one is justified [*made righteousness*] by faith apart from works of the law.   (Rom. 3:21-28 ESV)

[a]Note: *justified*, GK *dikaioo*, same root word for *righteousness*. This is righteousness that is imputed to the believer through genuine saving faith in Jesus as Lord and Savior.[2 Cor. 5:21; Phil. 3:9]

However, all those who have **not** yet genuinely trusted in Jesus as Lord and Savior remain under the wrath of God.[John 3:18, 36] Listen carefully, at the Great White Throne Judgment, people are not judged to see if they made it into Heaven. **If anyone's name that is not written down in the book of life**, they will be thrown into the Lake of Fire, Hell.

[12]And I saw the dead, small and great, standing before God, and books were opened. And **another book was opened, which is *the BOOK* OF LIFE**. And the dead were judged according to their works, by the things which were written in the books. [13]The sea gave up the dead who were in it, and Death and Hades delivered up the dead who were in them. And they were judged, each one according to his works. [14]Then Death and Hades were cast into the lake of fire. This is the second death. [15]And **anyone [*everyone's name*] not found written in the BOOK OF LIFE was cast into the lake of fire.**   (Rev. 20:12-15 NKJ)

The unregenerate are judged by the works to determine their degree in Hell. The unsaved are **not** judged to see if they made it into Heaven. The unredeemed are judged to determine their severity of the judgment in Hell. Remember,

The one who believes in him is not condemned. **The one who does not believe has been CONDEMNED ALREADY**, because he has not believed in the name of the one and only Son of God. (John 3:18 NET)

The Great White Throne Judgment is for all unregenerate, everyone without Christ as their personal Redeemer. No redeemed shall be present here at this judgment in Rev. 20:10ff. The saints will be judged for rewards or lost rewards, and this is at the Judgment Seat of Christ (the Bema Seat of Christ).[2 Cor. 5:10]

The believers were judged at the cross in Christ, and no believer shall be judged or condemned since we died in Christ.[John 5:24; Rom. 6:1-10; 8:1] However, it is possible that some saints may assist in at the Great White Throne Judgment. (Scripture is silent on this issue.) Still, the Great White Throne Judgment **is not** to determine whether one is lost or saved. The Great White Throne Judgment is to determine the **severity** or the **degree of punishment** for sin since they are without Christ as Lord and Savior. (Please read Rev. 20:12-15 again).

Every person's name that is **not** written in the BOOK OF LIFE is thrown into Hell. "And if anyone's name **was not** found written **in the BOOK OF LIFE**, he was thrown into the lake of fire."[Rev. 20:15] We have our names written in the Book of Life when we genuinely born from above by the Spirit of God! Friend, make sure your name is written down in the BOOK OF LIFE by trust and receiving Christ as Lord and Savior. Also, please make certain that your loved-ones are saved and have their names written down in heaven. No one can enter the Kingdom of God unless they are born from above through genuine saving faith in the Christ as Lord and only Savior. Therefore, trust and receive Jesus as your Lord and Savior right now.

B. The blessings are truly incalculable

The Bible says,

> Blessed be the God and Father of our Lord Jesus Christ, who **has blessed us in Christ with every spiritual blessing IN THE HEAVENLY PLACES**, [4]just as he chose us in Christ before the foundation of the world to be holy and blameless before him in love. [5]He destined us for adoption as his children through Jesus Christ, according to the good pleasure of his will, [6]to the praise of his glorious grace that he freely bestowed on us in the Beloved. [7]In him we have redemption through his blood, the forgiveness of our trespasses, according to the riches of his grace. (Eph. 1:3-7 NRS)

Even more abundant **blessings await us in Heaven** as Peter said, as we have noted previously.

> Blessed *be* the God and Father of our Lord Jesus Christ, which according to his abundant mercy hath begotten us again unto a lively hope by the resurrection of Jesus Christ from the dead, [4]To **an inheritance incorruptible**, and **undefiled**, and that *fade* **not away, RESERVED IN HEAVEN FOR YOU**, [5]Who are kept by the power of God through faith unto salvation ready to be revealed in the last time. [6]Wherein ye

greatly rejoice, though now for a season, if need be, ye are in heaviness through manifold temptations: [7]That the trial of your faith, being much more precious than of gold that *perishes*, though it be tried with fire, might be found unto praise and *honor* and glory at the appearing of Jesus Christ: [8]Whom having not seen, ye love; in whom, though now ye see *him* not, yet believing, ye rejoice with joy unspeakable and full of glory: [9]Receiving the end of your faith, *even* the salvation of *your* souls.   (1 Peter 1:3-9 KJV)

There are blessings awaiting the redeemed in Heaven. Ah, but Heaven is also a safe place for investment as well. True! It is wise to invest in Heaven in this life. Hello! Invest wisely now in Heaven? How can we invest in Heaven in this life? Regardless of how well your investments do in this life, at death, it shall all be left behind. Have you forgotten what Jesus said,

Lay not up for yourselves treasures upon earth, where moth and rust doth corrupt, and where thieves break through and steal: [20]But lay up for yourselves treasures in heaven, where neither moth nor rust doth corrupt, and where thieves do not break through nor steal: [21]For where your treasure is, there will your heart be also.   (Matt. 6:19-21 KJV)

Many do not believe the exhortation by our Lord since many do not even give ten percent, a tithe. They hog all their wealth upon the carnal things of this life, which are to perish. Yet, some of these people allege, "Oh, how I love Jesus." Really? Our Lord gives us the parable to illustrate investing in heaven in Christ.

[16]He spoke a parable to them, saying, "The ground of a certain rich man produced abundantly. [17]He reasoned within himself, saying, 'What will I do, because I don't have room to store my crops?' [18]He said, 'This is what I will do. I will pull down my barns, build bigger ones, and there I will store all my grain and my goods. [19]I will tell my soul, "Soul, you have many goods laid up for many years. Take your ease, eat, drink, and be merry.'" [20]But God said to him, '**You foolish one, tonight your soul is required of you**. The things which you have prepared—whose will they be?' [21]So is he who lays up treasure for himself, and is not rich toward God."   (Luke 12:16-21 WEB)

Pastor, let me first ask you this question? Are you rich in giving to the Lord's work including mission? I am talking about money coming out of your personal income; I am not talking money that comes from the church's revenue? Are you hogging most of your income for yourself? The truth is that many **do not believe what our Lord Jesus** said. Well, do you really believe Jesus who instructs us:

> Lay not up for yourselves treasures upon earth, where moth and rust doth corrupt, and where thieves break through and steal: [20]But lay up for yourselves treasures in heaven, where neither moth nor rust doth corrupt, and where thieves do not break through nor steal: [21]For where your treasure is, there will your heart be also.   (Matt. 6:19-21 KJV)

If we truly loved the Lord, don't you think it should be evident in our personal giving? So, if many Pastors do not give generously to the Lord, it is clear they do not believe what Jesus said in Matt. 6:19ff, and maybe their love is more for this world rather their love for Him. However, I warn you,

> But if any provide not for his own, and *especially* for those of his own house, he hath denied the faith, and is worse than an infidel.
>
> (1 Tim. 5:8 KJV)

The same with many people in the church. Unfortunately, many Christians err not knowing tithing predates the Mosaic Law. Tithing is a principle of creation. Abraham give a tithe to Melchizedek.[Gen. 14:18-20 (Heb. 7:1-19)] The fact that Hebrews uses the tithe, it applies to the church.

I wish to give you a lesson on Jacob while he was traveling over the mountains to some of his kin. Travel was very dangerous in those days. The text is slight long, but it is very important to read.

> [11]He [*Jacob*] came to a certain place and spent the night there, because the sun had set; and he took one of the stones of the place and put it under his head, and lay down in that place. [12]He had a dream, and behold, a ladder was set on the earth with its top reaching to heaven; and behold, the angels of God were ascending and descending on it. [13]And behold, the LORD [*a theophany of Christ*] stood above it and said, "I am the LORD, the God of your father Abraham and the God of Isaac; the land on which you lie, I will give it to you and to your descendants. [14]Your descendants will also be like the dust of the earth, and you will spread out to the west and to the east and to the north and to the south; and in you and in your descendants shall all the families of the earth be blessed. [15]Behold, I am with you and will keep you wherever you go, and will bring you back to this land; for I will not leave you until I have done what I have promised you."

¹⁶Then Jacob awoke from his sleep and said, "Surely the LORD is in this place, and I did not know it." ¹⁷He was afraid and said, "How awesome is this place! This is none other than **the house of God**, and this is the gate [*a door*] of heaven." ¹⁸So Jacob rose early in the morning, and took the stone that he had put under his head and set it up as a pillar and poured oil on its top. ¹⁹He called the name of that place **Bethel** [HEB, meaning "*the House of God*"]; however, previously the name of the city had been Luz.

²⁰Then **Jacob made a vow**, saying, "If God will be with me and will keep me [*safe*] on this journey that I take, and will give me food to eat and garments to wear, ²¹and I return to my father's house in safety, then **the LORD will be my God**. ²²"This stone, which I have set up as a pillar, will be **God's house**, and of **ALL THAT YOU GIVE ME I WILL SURELY GIVE A TENTH TO YOU**."   (Gen. 28:11-22)

Jacob did **not** ask for *wealth*. Jacob did **not** ask for *good health*. Jacob did **not** ask for *prosperity*. He only asked for: **protection**, **food**, **clothing**, and **return safely** to his father's house. Who dares to make such vow of a tithe for life today? Where are the men of faith today?

The point I wish us to see is that the saints cannot out give to the Lord whether it is worship, acts of mercy to others, giving to a godly church, to mission, or anything in the blessed Name Jesus. The Lord will bless you. The Lord will bless you, but unfortunately, the blessings will not be like the liars of the "*Name it and claim it*" of many Charismatics and many Pentecostals falsely espouse. We cannot out give the Lord. If you believe that, then, "put your money where your mouth is.²"

Well, many say, "I believe what Jesus says." Then prove it; for He said,

Give, and it will be given to you. A good measure, pressed down, shaken together, running over, will be put into your lap; for the measure you give will be the measure you get back."   (Luke 6:38 NRS)

Well, my friend, do you really believe what Jesus said? May you watch out also for hyper-dispensationalists who do not see such above text as a horizontal truth, which runs through the Bible. But if you truly believe such promises are true, then, "put your money where your mouth is."

Conclusion

However, I warn you that if you do not do the things for the Lord, but instead you do things more to receive the praise of men, then you have your reward already. Jesus says,

> "Be careful not to practice your righteousness in front of others to be seen by them. If you do, you will have no reward from your Father in heaven.
>
> (Matt. 6:1 NIV)

Keep in mind, many things done for Christ are based upon the carnal natural (the flesh, the old nature) and not in the Spirit. Then, all your service for Jesus will go up in smoke! The Bible says,

> For we are co-workers in God's service; you are God's field, God's building. [10]By the grace God has given me, I laid a foundation as a wise builder, and someone else is building on it. But each one should build with care. [11]For no one can lay any foundation other than the one already laid, which is Jesus Christ. [12]If anyone builds on this foundation using gold, silver, costly stones, wood, hay or straw, [13]their work will be shown for what it is, because the Day will bring it to light. It will be revealed with fire, and the fire will test the quality of each person's work. [14]If what has been built survives, the builder will receive a reward. [15]If it is burned up, the builder will suffer loss but yet will be saved— even though only as one escaping through the flames. [16]Don't you know that you yourselves are God's temple and that God's Spirit dwells in your midst? [17]If anyone destroys God's temple, God will destroy that person; for God's temple is sacred, and you together are that temple.
>
> (1 Cor. 3:9-17 NIV)

Yes indeed, there are rewards and blessings for those who are faithful. However, the Lord will reward those who labored honestly and by standards and rules of God. If anyone seeks to build according to their standards and rules, they may be shocked to see everything was built by the carnal natural and not the standards and rules by the Spirit of the living God. Liars and sheep-stealers will have no rewards. Others did the labor for which they shall receive a reward. Some shall have their reward already in this life. This is because they sought the praise of men, but they were not seeking the praises of the Lord our God.

The charlatans, the fake healers, and counterfeit preachers and teachers will find out soon enough. Woe unto those who only used the ministry for their own gain. Jesus said,

> The one who had received the five talents came and brought five more, saying, 'Sir, you entrusted me with five talents. See, I have gained five more [talents].' [21]His master answered, **'Well done, good and faithful slave**! You have been faithful in a few things. I will put you in charge of

many things. Enter into the joy of your master.' ²²The one with the two talents also came and said, 'Sir, you entrusted two talents to me. See, I have gained two more [*talents*].' ²³His master answered, **'Well done, good and faithful slave!** You have been faithful with a few things. I will put you in charge of many things. Enter into the joy of your master.' ²⁴Then the one who had received the one talent came and said, 'Sir, I knew that you were a hard man, harvesting where you did not sow, and gathering where you did not scatter seed, ²⁵so I was afraid, and I went and hid your talent in the ground. See, you have what is yours.' ²⁶But his master answered, **'Evil and lazy slave!** So you knew that I harvest where I didn't sow and gather where I didn't scatter? ²⁷Then you should have deposited my money with the bankers, and on my return I would have received my money back with interest! ²⁸Therefore take the talent from him and give it to the one who has ten. ²⁹For the one who has will be given more, and he will have more than enough. But the one who does not have, even what he has will be taken from him. ³⁰And throw that worthless slave into the outer darkness, where there will be weeping and gnashing of teeth.'   (Matt. 25:20-30 NET)

Friend, will you have any crowns to lay at the feet of the Savior? (This parable shall be discussed later since the parable has been abused and seriously misinterpreted by some Pastors.)

Footnotes:

1. "Propitiatory," Rom. 3:25: the GK *hilasterion*, is an extremely important word in the doctrine of redemption. *Hilasterion* points to the *mercy-seat* into the holy of holies. Christ's sacrifice on the cross placated or satisfied the holy and righteous demands for sin. There are two things involved in redemption for sins, but unfortunately, sometimes certain aspects in the doctrine of redemption is overlooked. First, there is the **placating for sin** of the sinner before a holy and righteous God for sin of the believer. (There is no placation for sin for the unbeliever.) Second, and equally important, is the **placating of the wrath of God against the sinner himself and his acts of rebellion.** Hence, there is the appeasement for the infinite consequences of the transgression against an infinitely holy and righteous God. The sacrifice of the Lord Jesus on the cross, His shed blood and death is available to all that genuinely believer and receive Christ Jesus as Lord and Savior.

My little children, I am writing these things to you so that you may not sin. And if anyone sins, we have an Advocate with the Father, Jesus Christ the righteous; and He **Himself is the propitiation for our sins**, and not for ours [sins] only, but also **for** [sinner and his sins] *those of* **the whole world**.   (1 John 2:1, 2 LSB)

2. "Put your money where your mouth is:" the meaning implied here is do what you say you will do. As given by Cambridge Dictionary: "to show by your actions and not just your words that you support or believe in something."

    https://dictionary.cambridge.org/us/dictionary/english/put-money-where-mouth-is#google_vignette

Part Three

Absence of God's Presence
but only condemnation

CHAPTER 9

The Door into Eternal Wrath

Memory verse

"Do not fear those who kill the body but are unable to kill the soul; but rather fear Him who is able to destroy both soul and body in hell."

(Matt. 10:28)

Introduction

Well-known *"Prosperity Gospel Preacher"* was asked if he fear God? He held out his *forefinger and thumb about two inches apart*, and then, he said, "About this much." He implied extremely *arrogantly* and *contemptuously* that he had no fear of God.

If you think the *Prosperity Preacher* was bad, what will you say about the *atheist, agnostic, secular-minded,* and the *intellectual* that rejects God or neatly placed Him in a box or put Him out of sight so that He no longer exist?

In a psalm, which is a psalm of King David, he says,

> The fool has said in his heart, "There is no God," They are corrupt, and have committed abominable injustice; There is no one who does good. [2] God has looked down from heaven upon the sons of men To see if there is anyone who understands, Who seeks after God. [3] Every one of them has turned aside; together they have become corrupt; There is no one who does good, not even one. (Psa. 53:1-3)

Unfortunately, the above sentiment exists in the religious world. This is because religion is *plastic*; it is synthetic, or manmade. Nowadays, it is so popular to refer to the Lord our God as *"god."* Even Christians are being generic when referring to the Lord God, the Creator and Sustainer of everything that lives and breathes. (Tragically, many Christians do not even know the difference between the name "**LORD**" and the word "God," whether OT or NT.) Many today are like the foolish *Prosperity Gospel Preacher* that held out his forefinger and thumb about two inches apart to demonstrate that he had no fear of God. However, let us once again note the memory verse as our Lord said,

> "Do not fear those who kill the body but are unable to kill the soul; but rather fear Him who is able to destroy both soul and body in hell."

> (Matt. 10:28)

Even among Fundamentalists and Evangelicals, it is popular to think of God with *reverence* rather than **fear**. Certainly, we need to have *reverence* for God since He is indeed a holy and righteous God. However, the word "*reverence*" is insufficient to properly describe what is declaring in Matt. 10:28.

However, for the moment, let us consider the Seraph angels once again that fly in the present of the Lord. Seraphs covered themselves with four wings in the presence of the Lord God Almighty. Then, the Seraphim cry out loud "Holy, Holy, and Holy."[Isa. 6:2-4] Was the Seraphim action just out of reverence or something much more?

Similarly, Isaiah said,

> And I said, Woe is me, for I am pricked to the heart; for being a man, and having unclean lips, I dwell in the midst of a people having unclean lips; and I have seen with mine eyes the King, the Lord of hosts.

> (Isa. 6:5 LXE)

Remember, when the high priest entered the holy of holies (which was only a copy of real one), it is said that a rope was tied to his foot. The rope to the foot was in case he is struck dead while he was in the holy of holies. The end of the rope outside the holy of holies was used to pull him out. Did they do this out of just reverence or fear?

Once again, the apostle John is caught up in a vision into the presence of the risen Lord Jesus, the Lord of Glory, and John says,

> When I saw Him, **I FELL AT HIS FEET LIKE A DEAD**[a] **MAN**. And He placed His right hand on me, saying, "Do not be afraid; I am the first and the last."　　　　　(Rev. 1:17)

> [a]Note: John fell as a dead; he was *petrified* with fear in the present of risen and glorified Lord.

88

Hear me, many at the Great White Throne Judgment will indeed be like Nabal, the husband of Abigail. Nabal initially and foolishly insulted and refused to offer assistance to David and his furious fighting men in time need. When Nabal awoke from his drunken stupor, Abigail informed him of whom he had really insulted and refused assistance. Nabal had refused the mighty King David, and David and his men had protected Nabal's livestock. Abigail warned him to anticipation the wrath of the King due ungodly behavior against the King. Then, we read,

> But in the morning, when the wine had gone out of Nabal, his wife told him these things, and **his heart died within him so that he became** *like* **a stone**. (1 Sam. 25:37)

Friend, Nabal's experience is what should be called *petrified fear*. I am warning you; so, listen carefully, the Bible says,

> The fear of the LORD *is* the beginning of knowledge: *but* fools despise wisdom and instruction. (Prov. 1:7 KJV)

If you still think that the key word in Matt. 10:28 still means *"reverence"* rather than *"fear,"* my friend you are in for a **rude awakening**! Yet, this is attitude in many churches today. If this is the attitude of many churches, how much more the world at large? The Lord our God is indeed a consuming fire.[Heb. 12:29]

A. It is a lake of eternal fire

The problem facing the churches today is that the pulpit is vacant of *bold* and *valiant* men full of faith, obedience, prayer, and sealed with *unwavering integrity* to the Word and *obedient* to the Spirit of God. (How shall people be obedient if they do not do and practice?[2 Tim. 2:15]) Churches are running on secularism, humanism, intellectualism, and engulfed with materialism. Jesus and His mandates are **abandoned** and **discarded**. Sadly, some do not even know what our Lord's mandates are. How spiritual putrid is that? They just assume arrogantly, they can do anything they want.

Listen, don't you know we get our orders from on High? We do not give orders to Heaven. Again, *"We do not give orders to Heaven;"* Heaven gives us orders. My friend, I am telling you, we had better wake up; Jesus' coming is sooner than most of us can even imagine.

There is no cry out to warn people of the pending infinite wrath of God, which is coming without mercy. There is more concern for their popularity, tolerance, and what is in the bank account rather than hearing, 'Well done thou good and faithful servant.' For shame!

Yet, many in the pulpit know or ought to know that the infinite wrath and furious anger of God is going to be poured out without measure upon the unregenerate. Everyone that has not been born from above by genuine saving faith in the risen Lord Jesus will perish in Hell. Yes, the redeemed have been washed, justified, indwelt, sanctified, and sealed by the Holy Spirit.[1 Cor. 6:9-11]

The psalmist said concerning the dreadful wrath of God,

> [7]You, You [*Lord*] *indeed* are to be feared, And who may stand in Your presence, once You are angry? [8]You [*Lord*] caused judgment to be heard from heaven; The earth feared and was still [9]When God arose to judgment, To save all the humble of the earth. Selah [10]For the wrath of mankind shall praise You [*Lord*]; You will encircle Yourself with a remnant of wrath. (Psa. 76:7-10)

Where are the fearless men of faith like Jonathan Edwards that preached "Sinners in the hands of an angry God?" Yes, the churches had forsaken the blessed Gospel and His mandates. This is the Gospel that warns the sinner to repent and turn to Jesus Christ. The unregenerate need to make a total commitment and completely trust with genuine saving faith in the risen Lord of glory, or else, they shall surely perish in their sins forever and ever.

The Word of God continually warns the world of the coming wrath of God. Please listen, this is no metaphor. The pending infinite and dreadful wrath of God is coming upon everyone whose names are not written in the book of life.

> If[b] anyone's name was not found written in the book of life, that person was thrown into the lake of fire. (Rev. 20:15 NET)

> [b]Note: NET gives the comment to the omission of "*And*, GK kai." The NET note on v 15 reads, "Here καί (*kai*) has not been translated because of differences between Greek and English style."

The apostle John uses the phrase, 'the lake of fire.'[Rev. 20:15] Nevertheless, the lake of fire is infinite in size, suffering, and duration. The Lord Jesus warns those who only have *a profession of faith* but **void genuine saving faith**. Meaning a person had better be certain that they have been regeneration by the Holy Spirit.[2 Cor. 13:5]

This is indeed a serious warning to any person without regeneration by the Holy Spirit. That is, this a warning to any person that is void of possessing genuine commitment and trust in Christ as Lord. A person must be trusting in Jesus' redemption on the cross. If they are truly saved in Christ, they ought to exhibit a changed life produced by the Holy Spirit indwelling them. We do not change ourselves to get to Heaven. The change must come from the living God within the believer.

> [42]But if anyone causes one of these little ones who believe in Me to stumble [e.g., in their faith in Christ], it would be better for him to have a millstone hung around his neck and to be thrown into the sea. [43] If your hand causes you to sin, cut it off. It is better for you to enter life crippled than to have two hands and go into hell[c], into the **unquenchable fire**, [44]where 'their **worm never dies**, and the **fire is never quenched**.' [45]If your foot causes you to sin, cut it off. It is better for you to enter life lame than to have two feet and be thrown into hell, into the **unquenchable fire**, [46]where 'their **worm never dies**, and the **fire is never quenched**.' [47]And if your eye causes you to sin, pluck it out. It is better for you to enter the kingdom of God with one eye than to have two eyes and be thrown into the fire of hell, [48]where 'their **worm never dies**, and the **fire is never quenched**.' (Mark 9:42-48 MBS)

> [c]Note: hell is the GK word Gehenna; HEB "GEY'HINNOM-" *the valley wailing*. It is also said to be where garbage was dumped outside Jerusalem. The garbage was continually burning; yet, one could see worms crawling throughout the garbage. What dreadful portrait of hell.

> *"Cut it off"* a *hand*, a *foot*, or "pluck it out" an *eye*, is a hyperbole or an extreme emphasis. This is to drive a major point to make sure you are in the faith of Christ. It is not to be taken literally. Jesus is not saying e.g., '*Cut off your hand*' or '*pluck out your eye*.'

The below warning comes from Isaiah that says,

> And they shall go forth, and see the carcasses of the men that have transgressed against me: for **their worm shall not die**, and **their fire shall not be quenched**; and they shall be a spectacle to all flesh.
>
> (Isa. 66:24 LXE)

Friend, I am warning you that the Lake of Fire is real. The Lake of Fire is forever and ever. Make certain you and your loved-ones are indeed in the faith of the Lord Jesus Christ. Everyone that is not in Christ shall perish in their sins in Hell, where the *worm shall not die* and the *fire shall not be quenched*. There will be no mercy for those outside the redemption through faith in Jesus Christ.

Everyone without Jesus Christ as your Lord and only Savior shall enter the door to eternal wrath of God. This is no retrieve; there is no turning back once one enters the door into eternity. Right now, today, is the day of salvation. Believe on the Lord Jesus and you shall be saved.^{Acts 16:31}

B. Alive in your body and soul

Once again, please let us examine the graphic scene at the Great White Throne Judgment. This is a terrifying and horrifying description of fallen angels (evil angels) and every person that is lost in sin and without Christ as their personal Savior. Friend, let's tremble for there is no appeal; they will spend eternity in Hell

> The devil, who deceived them, was cast into the lake of fire and brimstone where the beast and the false prophet, ^[Rev. 19:20] *are*. And they will be tormented day and night forever and ever. ¹¹Then I saw a great white throne and Him who sat on it, from whose face the earth and the heaven fled away. And there was found no place for them. ¹²And I saw the dead, small and great, standing before God, and books were opened. And another book was opened, which is *the Book* of Life. And the dead were judged according to their works, by the things which were written in the books. ¹³The sea gave up the dead who were in it, and Death and Hades delivered up the dead who were in them. And they were judged, each one according to his works. ¹⁴Then Death and Hades were cast into the lake of fire. This is the second death. ¹⁵And anyone not found written in the Book of Life was cast into the lake of fire. (Rev. 20:10-15 NKJ)

All the evil angels are judged at the same time as the devil. The *beast* and *false prophet* were cast into the Lake Fire before the thousand-years reign of Christ. Does this suggest that the *beast* and *false prophet* were really evil spirits and not humans? There is no redemption for evil angels. Hell was prepared for the evil angels.

> "Then He will also say to those on His left, 'Depart from Me, accursed ones, into the eternal fire which has been prepared for the devil and his angels   (Matt. 25:41)

Angels were individually created. The angels that sinned, they sinned individually. There is no redemption for angels that sinned.

[14]Forasmuch then as the children are partakers of flesh and blood, he also himself likewise took part of the same; that through death he might <u>destroy</u> [b] him that had the power of death, that is, the devil; [15] And deliver them who through fear of death were all their lifetime subject to bondage. [16] For verily he took not on *him the nature of* angels; but he took on *him* the seed of Abraham. Heb. 2:14-16 KJV	[14]*Just as humans are flesh and blood, Christ took on a human nature as a man. Through His sacrificial death, Christ rendered <u>powerless</u>, [b]that is, the devil that kept people in fear of death.* [15]*Christ delivered His people from the fear and life of bondage.* [16] *For He did not take on the nature of angels, but He took on Abraham's seed [as a man to redeem us].*Gal. 3:26-29 Heb. 2:14-16 paraphrased

[b]Note: ENG word "*destroy*" is GK *katargeo*. *Katargeo* does **NOT** mean to *erase* or *obliterate*. GK lex. says, the word means to make *powerless, inoperative, ineffective,* or *non-effect*. The devil has no power of death over anyone.

Some hyper-dispensationalists argue that Hebrews Epistle is not for the church. This is nonsense to say Hebrews is not for church. The church is joint heirs with all the redeemed.Eph. 2:14ff However, as joint heirs in Christ does not diminish Israel's future fulfillment, promises, and blessings. Postmillennialism and Amillennialism has erred by spiritualizing OT promises to the church. Many of the OT promises were unconditional and sealed by the promises of God. God who cannot lie! He shall surely fulfill His promises to Israel.Matt. 5:17, 18; Titus 1:2; Heb. 6:18-20 God will fulfill every word, but not because Israel or the church is faithful. The Lord our God who made the promise, He is faithful.1 Thess. 5:24 Hallelujah!

As to angels, the holy angels are *created* and *sealed* in absolute holiness and righteousness. Holy angels remained faithful; whereas, other angels chose to follow Lucifer in rebellion and sinned. Therefore, the angels that sinned were stripped of all holiness and righteousness, and those angels that sinned became *total evil* and *void of any redeeming good*. Let me also tell you that there was only one fall of angels (not two), which was a time testing all of creation.

God in His infinite wisdom decided to provide redemption for Adam's posterity, the human race. Angels were individually created. Also, angels are incapable of reproducing or procreating themselves like Adam's race. Angels had no need to reproduce. God created all the various angels He ever wanted or needed.

Adam's posterity is a race. As a race, man is able procreate himself. Unlike angels which were individually created, having no need to procreate. Our Lord tabernacles Himself in flesh and blood. He became fully human. Thus, in the incarnation, Christ the Lord is fully God and He is also fully human in one person.

> Without controversy, the mystery of godliness is great: God[d] was revealed in the flesh, justified in the spirit, seen by angels, preached among the nations, believed on in the world, and received up in glory. (1 Tim. 3:16 WEB)

[d]Note: some GK MSS only "*He*."

When discussing the hypostatic Union (the union of Christ's Deity and human nature), we must be very, very careful. The Lord cannot be less than who He is. He remains Almighty God in the flesh, and He remains Almighty forever though He possesses human body.

The Lord changes not; He is the same forever.[Mal. 3:6; James 1:17; Heb. 13:8] The Lord is Eternal God, without beginning and end. The Lord is from everlasting to everlasting. Yet, God tabernacles Himself as a human, being fully man. Thus, Jesus possessed two distinct natures, God and man, in one person, Jesus Christ. These two natures were never compromised, mingled, impeded, distorted, or mixed. The two natures (Eternal God and fully human) remain separate and distinct.

As Christ the Lord was prophesied to tabernacle in flesh, Isaiah said,

> For unto us a Child is born, Unto us a Son is given; And the government will be upon His shoulder. And **His name will be** called **Wonderful, Counselor, Mighty God, Everlasting Father**[e], **Prince of Peace**.
>
> (Isa. 9:6 NKJ)

[e]Note: the meaning of "Everlasting Father" is implying that the Messiah or the Christ is the Creator of all things. Christ is not the Father in reference to the Trinity. The Trinity share in one essence of being, but Trinity is in the Person: the Father, the Son, and the Holy Spirit.

In the GK, Jesus said as literally translated by the Aramaic Bible in Plain ENG,

> "I and my Father, **We are One**."　　　　　(John 10:30 ABPE)

The expression is:

> GK: Ego kai o' pater 'en esmen[f]. (BYZ)

ENG: I and the Father we are one.

'Note: GK word "*esmen*" is the word "*we are*;" this understood but not translated.

Therefore, Christ the Lord is Almighty God from everlasting to everlasting. Christ is the Designer, Creator, and Sustainer of all living things and all the universe.[John 1:1-3, 10; 1 Cor. 8:9; Col. 1:16f; Heb. 1:2]

Christ is Lord and Creator of all things; let us then be certain to heed Jesus' warning,

> "Do not fear those who kill the body but are unable to kill the soul; but rather fear Him who is able to destroy both soul and body in hell.
>
> (Matt. 10:28)

As we have noted,[Rev. 20:10-15] everyone that does not have their name written in the Book of Life is thrown into Hell, the Lake of Fire. Remember, Jesus said,

> Where 'their <u>worm</u> <u>never</u> <u>dies</u>, and the <u>fire</u> <u>is</u> <u>never</u> <u>quenched</u>.'
>
> (Mark 9:48 MBS)

Conclusion

Many people deny that Hell exists, but their denial does not diminish the dreadful reality of the wrath of God coming upon all sinners outside the redemption in Jesus. Heaven is **not** attainable through human works. There are none righteous. No, not even one.[Rom. 3:10-12]

No one will enter Heaven through religious rites (e.g., water baptism, last rites, or prayer for dead.) Such practices are wicked and pagan. "Just as people are destined to die once, and after that to face judgment."[Heb. 9:27 NIV] No religion or religious pietism can take away or remove sin.

The apostle Paul is very clear that we are saved through faith in Christ and His mercy and grace alone.

> For we also once were foolish, disobedient, deceived, serving divers lusts and pleasures, living in malice and envy, hateful, hating one another. [4]But when the kindness of God our *Savior*, and his love toward man [*humanity*], appeared, [5]not by works *done* in righteousness, which we did ourselves, but according to his mercy he saved us, through the washing of regeneration and renewing of the Holy Spirit, [6]which he poured out upon us richly, through Jesus Christ our *Savior*; [7]that, being

justified [*made righteous*] by his grace, we might be made heirs according to the hope of eternal life. ⁸Faithful is the saying, and concerning these things I desire that thou affirm confidently, to the end that they who have believed God may be careful to maintain good works. These things are good and profitable unto men: (Titus 3:3-8 ASV)

My friend, I must warn you again that unless you have been genuinely born from above [John 3:3-7] through the commitment and trust in Jesus as your personal Lord and only Savior, you will surely perish in Hell forever and ever. Call on Jesus as Lord right now, and He will save you from your sins.[John 1:12; 5:24; Rom. 10:9-13]

It is a terrifying thing to fall into the hands of the living God. (Heb. 10:31)

CHAPTER 10

Errors to enter Heaven's Gate, escaping Hell

SECTION 1:
Universalism to Religious Rites

Memory verse

This is good and acceptable in the sight of God our Savior, who desires all men to be saved and to come to the knowledge of the truth.

(1 Tim. 2:3, 4)

Introduction

The churches are plagued and flooded with every kind of false doctrines. Still, new defective doctrines continue to emerge with the wild speculation. This is the result of the human depraved mind which is alienated and without illumination from God. So, it is impossible to examine every false doctrine that arises with carnal and depraved minds today. Hell is very real. Unfortunately, many will miss out on receiving the free gift of eternal life in Christ. Let us warn everyone but especially those who desire to go to Heaven. Heaven's Gate is only through genuine saving faith in Christ as Lord, and without Jesus as Lord and Savior, their abode is in Hell.

Let us note some defective or false doctrines related the biblical teaching of salvation into Heaven. A complete volume devoted this topic would probably be insufficient since, as I have said, new false doctrines continue to emerge seemingly with no end in sight. I have written two chapters covering these issues, *Errors to enter Heaven's Gate, escaping Hell*. Hopefully, the samplings will help cover many of the misnomers and misconceptions of how people think they can enter Heaven and escape the fires of Hell.

A. Universalism
B. There is the elect and non-elect
C. All religions are the same
D. Religious rites
E. Sufficient good works
F. Sincerity is sufficient
G. Canned confession
H. Denial of Hell

The doctrine of Hell is frightening subject. Yet, our Lord Jesus spoke on Hell more so than anyone else in the Bible. So, because our Lord spoke on Hell more than anyone else, it is indeed an important topic to discuss. Hell is terrifying, and many of us get uneasy when the topic is presented. Friend, if you are feel uneasy in the discussion of Hell, that is a good thing and spiritual healthy.

Yet, God's desire is that people are saved, and the Lord does not desire anyone to perish in their sin. Sadly, many will perish in their sin. Many people will enter eternity without Christ as Lord and Savior and perish in their sin. Nevertheless, the Lord our God is beyond infinity in holiness and righteousness. (God is beyond measure of time, space, and matter, and He is beyond infinity of all things.) Because of God's holiness and righteousness, sin shall be reckoned or dealt with by God.

A. Universalism

By definition, "universalism" is the belief that everyone shall be saved, even the devil is believed to be saved in the doctrine of universalism. The doctrine of universalism is taught by cults and other false religious sects in Christendom. Still others often assume that the deceased person is now in Heaven. Platitudes given at grave sites leave the impression that most people at death made it to Heaven. Well, such words at committal service is comforting to the bereaved, but it is a lie. Unfortunately, it is assumed that most of the departed dead went to Heaven. However, the dreadful reality is that the majority of people will end up in Hell forever and ever. Jesus said,

> "Enter through the narrow gate; for the gate is wide and the way is broad that leads to destruction, and there are many who enter through it [wide gate to destruction]. For the gate is small and the way is **narrow that**

leads to life, and <u>**THERE**</u> <u>**ARE**</u> <u>**FEW**</u> <u>**WHO**</u> <u>**FIND**</u> <u>**IT**</u>. **Beware of the false prophets**, who come to you in sheep's clothing, but inwardly are ravenous wolves." (Matt. 7:13-15)

It is a fact that the road to Hell is full with most people. The road to Hell is full because some who profess faith in Christ are not genuinely born above by the Holy Spirit. Listen, many people will end up in Hell even though people do not want end up in Hell. Even though many reject or deny the existence of Hell, many still fear the concept of the existence of a Hell. Whether people acknowledge Hell or not, Hell is indeed a very real place. It is very evident that those who acknowledge there is Hell do not want to go there. What a contradiction this leaves with many people.

At the grave site, people may give platitudes of comforting words to the bystanders, but the truth is majority of people are going end up in Hell. Yet, no one need to go to Hell regardless of the sin or wickedness. This is why we must warn people now in this life and before the door into eternity opens for each of us, one by one. Remember, God's Word declares,

And as it is appointed unto men once to die, but after this the judgment:

(Heb. 9:27 KJV)

Amillennialism and Postmillennialism deny the thousand-year reign of Jesus Christ in Rev. 201ff. Still, this does not change anything. There is indeed a reign of Christ on earth. His reign shall prove that peace, justice, tranquility, and even ecosystem can be achieved in this old world. The evil that humankind has done to one another, justice will be served. Since there is a thousand-year reign by our Lord on earth, the unsaved will wait for the judgment in Hades. [Luke 16:19-31] They wait in Hades until the Great White Throne Judgment. [Rev. 20:10-15] Friend, the text in Rev. 20:10ff is literally true. Nevertheless, the judgment and His wrath are indeed real, and it is coming at the end of the millennium.

Universalism is a lie. Most people will end up in Hell because they did not truly receive Jesus Lord and were void being born above by the Holy Spirit. Still, no one need be in Hell regardless of the severity and wickedness of sin. This is correct, no one need be in Hell if a person will genuinely turn to Jesus Christ. There is no religion or church that can deliver you from the penalty of sin, only Jesus can. Everyone must genuinely repent of their sin and make an unreserved commitment and trust Jesus as personal Lord and Savior who laid down His life on the cross for our sins.

Our Lord's sacrifice for sin is more than sufficient or efficacious to save everyone that ever lived, [John 3:16ff; 1 John 2:1, 2] Jesus death on the cross was for His redeemed. Christ died in particular on behalf of the believers. Therefore, you must personally trust and receive Him as your Lord and Savior.

In the Garden, Jesus did not pray a generalized prayer. In the Garden of Gethsemane, He prayed specifically for those who were to believe in Him.

> "I ask on their behalf [those that believe in Me]; I **do not** [pray in general] of the world, but [ask in particular] of those whom You have given Me; for they are Yours."
>
> (John 17:9)

Our Lord laid down His life for those who genuinely were to believe in Him unto eternal life. However, let me be very, very clear, Christ's sacrifice and His propitiation of sin is indeed available to everyone that genuinely trusts in Him as Lord and Savior.

> My little children, I am writing these things to you so that you may not sin. And if anyone sins, we have an Advocate [Counselor] with the Father, Jesus Christ the righteous; and He Himself is the propitiation for our sins; and not for ours only, but also for *those of* the whole world.
>
> (1 John 2:1, 2)

> The next day John *sees* Jesus coming unto him, and saith, Behold the Lamb of God, which taketh away the sin of the world. (Jn. 1:29 KJV)

Jesus was very clear concerning those who do not trust in Jesus as Lord and Savior as given by the International Standard Version 2012,

> "That is why I told you that you will die in your sins, for unless you believe that I AM[a], you'll die in your sins." (John 8:24 ISV)

> [a]Note: there is no "*He*" in the GK in [v 24]; but many translations assume that the "*He*" is implied. I do not think the "*He*" is implied. Jesus is referring to Himself as great "**I Am**" in Exodus 3:13-15, which is HEB name for **LORD**. E.g., the same is in John 8:58. In John 18:5, 6, the "*He*" is not in the GK. When Jesus said, "**I Am**" [John 18:6] the religious leaders fell to the ground.

Universalism is a serious and severe false doctrine. Jesus is clear that most people are on the broad way to destruction because they failed to make the commitment and trust in Christ, [Matt. 7:13-15].

B. The *Electionists*

One the greatest errors among Evangelicals and Fundamentalists is the extreme teaching and misunderstand of the biblical doctrine of election. First, (as it has already be said) when Christ died to save mankind, He did die particularly and exclusively for the redeemed. This is indeed a biblical fact. Our Lord did not die a generalized death. Yet, our Lord Jesus Christ's sacrifice for sin is **infinitely sufficient** and **available** for every person that ever lived in the world. Our Lord made no provision for redemption, so the angels rebelled and sinned.[Heb. 2:16] (The Universalists ignorantly and erroneously allege Christ died for evil angels, which is not true.) Once again, the apostle John says very clearly,

> My little children, these things write I unto you, that ye sin not. And if any man sin, we have an advocate with the Father, Jesus Christ the *Righteous* [*One*]: And **he is the propitiation**[b] **for our sins: and not for ours only, but also for** *the sins of* **the whole world.**
>
> (1 John 2:1, 2 KJV)

> [b]Note: the word <u>propitiation</u> is very strong word for redemption. Propitiation means Christ's sacrifice indeed completely satisfied the righteous demands for sin of humans. John's words are explicit, "- but also Christ's sacrifice for *the sins* is indeed sufficient for **THE WHOLE WORLD.**"

Hebrews is clear that our Lord tasted death for every person,

> But we do see Him who was made [e.g., *condescended*] for a little while lower than the angels, *namely*, Jesus, because of the suffering of death crowned with glory and honor, so that by the grace of God **He might taste death for everyone.** (Heb. 2:9)

Again, the apostle Paul says,

> [1]First of all, then, I urge that requests, **prayers**, **intercession,** *and* **thanksgiving** be made **in behalf of <u>ALL</u> <u>PEOPLE</u>,** [2]for kings and all who are in authority, so that we may lead a tranquil and quiet life in all godliness and dignity. [3]This is **GOOD and ACCEPTABLE** in the sight of God our Savior, [4]**who wants** [desires] **<u>ALL</u> <u>PEOPLE</u> TO BE SAVED** and **to COME TO THE KNOWLEDGE OF THE TRUTH.** [5]For there is one God, *and* one mediator also between God and mankind, *the* man **Christ Jesus,** [6]**WHO GAVE HIMSELF AS A RANSOM FOR ALL**, the testimony *given* at the proper time. (1 Tim. 2:1-6)

Again, the apostle Paul says,

> For to this end we toil and struggle, because we have **our hope set on the living God, WHO IS THE SAVIOR OF ALL PEOPLE**, especially of those who believe. (1 Tim. 4:10 NRS)

One of greatest verses in the Bible, and its context is very clear as to God's purpose for ALL MANKIND.

> And as Moses lifted up the serpent in the wilderness, even so must the Son of man be lifted up: [15]That **whosoever** *believes* **in him should not perish, but have eternal life.** [16]For **GOD SO LOVED THE WORLD**, that he gave his only begotten Son, that whosoever *believes* in him should not perish, but have everlasting life. [17]For God sent not his Son into the world to condemn the world; but that **the world through him might be saved.** [18]**He that** *believes* **on him is not condemned**: but he that *believes* not is condemned already, because he hath not believed in the name of the only begotten Son of God. (John 3:14-18 KJV)

Those who adamantly follow strict election maintain only the elect are able be saved. (I find it ironic the various disagreements among Calvinists and adamant Lutherans.) The Calvinists and Lutherans cannot agree among themselves even on the propitiatory sacrifice of our Lord. Some argue there is even a *double election*: God elected the redeemed, but God also elected the dammed. (Meaning that God "elected those who were to be dammed;" God elected all those who would be lost forever.) How quaint! Islam teaching is similar doctrine: Allah choose who may go to Heaven unless the person dies as a martyr in a *Jihad* or *holy war*.

Nevertheless, the Lord our God so loved the world. The meaning is not that the Lord love the world system; perish that thought, [1 John 2:15-17]. Moreover, the meaning is not that the Lord loved only the world of the elect, which is the eisegesis of electionists. Listen, the Lord loved humankind whom He made in His image and likeness. Watch out, [Deut. 4:12-20] Scripture is very clear man does not look like God nor does God look like His creation of man.

Electionists, do have one thing correct. Jesus did not die to generalize death for all people. Our Lord most definitely died in particular for His redeemed. Jesus is very clear in His High Priestly prayer in John 17.

> "I ask on their [the apostles] behalf; I **DO NOT** ask on behalf of the world, but of those whom You have given Me; for they are Yours; (John 17:9)

> "I do not pray for these [e.g., *apostles*] alone [it is not for their sake only that I make this request], but also for [all] those who [will ever] believe *and* trust in Me through their message." (John 17:20 AMP)

The world hates Jesus. True, this is because He exposes the wickedness of the world,[John 7:7; 15:18] and the world hates the followers of Christ.[John 15:18-27; 17:14] This is because the Lord Jesus and all faithful saints speak out against the wickedness of the world around us. Yet, despite the world hating Jesus, Christ's redemption is more than sufficient and available to everyone but particularly, those who believe in Him.[John 4:42; 1 Tim. 4:10; Titus 2:11] The offer of redemption is indeed available to anyone that truly commits their life and fully trusts Him as Lord and only Savior. Nevertheless, all those without genuinely receiving Christ Jesus Lord and Savior will surely perish forever in their sins.

C. All religions are the same

Let me say first and foremost, there is no religion that is able to remove sin and give eternal life. All religions are manmade, and such religions will only lead a person into Hell. So, ironically, all religions are the same. However, my friend, listen carefully, Christ is a *living* and *vibrant relationship* with living and eternal God; this is not religion.

The forgiveness of sin is found only in and through Jesus Christ as Lord and Savior. Even if one attends or is a member of an Evangelical or Fundamental church, this is cannot save him/her from their sins. The Bible is clear,

> "There is salvation in no one else, for there is no other name under heaven [*Jesus Christ*] given among mortals by which we must be saved." (Acts 4:12 NRS)

Salvation, the deliverance from the penalty of sin is unachievable by manmade religion. Religion is humanity's futile attempt to achieve forgiveness and reconciliation of a "god" of his own manufacturing. This is because in man's darken and depraved mind without Christ the Lord, mankind fails to understand and believe that he is alienated from God due his sin. Humanity is oblivious to what is the means or bases for reconciliation with the Lord.

Jesus was clear with Samaritan woman, '**You do not know what you worship**.'[John 4:22] If this is true of the Samaritan woman who had at least the Books of Moses as authority of Scripture, how much more the rest of the world today who do not believe or even have the Word of God? Unfortunately, there are many that have the Bible but they either do not read the Bible or they are in darkness following false religious leaders. Also, humanity is worshipping *a god* of their own manufacturing. The Word of God and His revelation was entrusted to faithful Jewish believers.[Rom. 3:1f; 9:4, 5] Without the Bible, OT and NT, we could not know God or know His will. Now the church, the body Christ, has been entrusted with the Word of God, ^{Jude 1:3}. Those churches giving out God Word and declaring the Bible everywhere faithfully is only a dribble.

Therefore, people that allege that all religions are the same, their assertion is correct. Religion is manmade and continues through human origin. Religion is mankind's effect to reach out to *a god* of his imagination. Humankind is in darkness, blinded, and following the course of the world. Man's darken and depraved mind is only leading him into an eternal Hell from where there is no turning back.

The Lord our God is the only One that can save anyone from our sin which separates us from Him due to our wickedness. There is no God but the Lord. If the Lord had not communicated to humankind through His Word, the Bible, we could never know the Creator. We could only surmise there is a God, but we could never know Him apart from His divine revelation, the Bible.

Without divine revelation given by the Lord God to mankind, we could never know Him or know His will and purpose for His creation. This is why we have the Bible given to us by God.^{Rom. 10:17} The Lord used over forty different biblical scribes to write down His revelation for the posterity of all mankind. Therefore, without the divine revelation, the Bible, given to us by God, man could only grope after God but never know Him or His will.

The Bible warns humankind in seeking God based on his natural sense and depraved reasoning. Proverbs says,

> There is a way that seems right to a person, but its end is the way that leads to death.　　　　　　　　　　　　　　　(Proverbs NET)

Please listen carefully to me. There are three major reasons no one ought to lean on his natural instincts or human feeling. While these three things are interwoven together, each of these deadly influences are separate and distinct from one another.

1. The **heart is bent on evil**. Simply meaning that man's nature is bent towards evil. Jesus said,

   > "For out of the heart proceed evil thoughts, murders, adulteries, fornications, thefts, false witness, blasphemies.　　(Matt. 15:19 NKJ)

Even when the flood was over, the Lord said concerning humankind,

> The LORD said in his heart, "I will never again curse the ground because of man, for **the intention of man's heart is evil from his youth**. Neither will I ever again strike down every living creature as I have done.　　　　　　　　　　　　　(Gen. 8:21 ESV)

104

2. The **world is** totally **corrupt** and **warped**, and man **distorts** the view of life. The Bible says,

> Do not love the world nor the things in the world. If anyone loves the world, the love of the Father is not in him. For all that is in the world, the lust of the flesh and the lust of the eyes and the boastful pride of life, is not from the Father, but is from the world. The world is passing away, and *also* its lusts; but the one who does the will of God lives forever.
>
> (1 John 2:15-17)

This world system is on a collision course into Hell. Many have been deceived imagining that the world around them is natural and without corruption.

> Ye adulterers and adulteresses, know ye not that the friendship of the world is enmity with God? whosoever therefore will be a friend of the world is the enemy of God. (James 4:4 KJV)

3. The **demonic forces** that are **blinding** and **leading people astray** from the truth, [2 Cor. 4:3f]. Nevertheless, the grace of God that brings salvation has indeed appeared to all mankind, [Titus2:11-13]. The Bible warns us of the cunning and deception of false teachers being energized by evil angels.

> For such men are false apostles, deceitful workers, disguising themselves as apostles of Christ. No wonder, for even Satan disguises himself as an angel of light. Therefore it is not surprising if his servants also disguise themselves as servants of righteousness, whose end will be according to their deeds. (2 Cor. 11:13-15)

D. Religious rites

There are endless religious rites, and the foolishness of humankind is trusting in these manmade rites to keep from going into Hell. However, they are trusting lies that were manufactured through manmade religions. There is no religious rite that is able to cleanse the soul of man. There is only the shed blood and death of Jesus Christ on the cross that can cleanse us of all our sins.

Man does not set the standard for righteousness into God's Heaven. This simple truth is easy to understand. Heaven belongs to God, and so, He alone sets the standard. Nevertheless, let us note some fallacies that religious groups have concocted.

Water baptism:

Millions are deceived and are depending on *water baptism* to remove sin. This is a lie, and anyone trusting in their *water baptism* will perish in their sin. The Bible is very clear,

> Then he called for a light, and sprang in, and came trembling, and fell down before Paul and Silas, And brought them out, and said, Sirs, what must I do to be saved? And they said, **Believe on the Lord Jesus Christ**, and thou shalt be saved, and thy house.   (Acts 16:29-31 KJV)

The question that needs to be asked: "Are you trusting solely in Christ and His redemption?" Without Christ Jesus as Lord and Savior of your life, you will surely perish in your sins.

Communion:

The consumption (eating of the *bread* and drinking of the *cup*) of the Lord's Supper or Communion, also known as the Eucharist, meaning Thanksgiving, does not forgive sin. Some people, who have been deceived and led astray by ecclesiastical traditions and dogma, allege they are eating flesh and drinking blood of Christ. Yes, Jesus said,

> "So Jesus said to them, 'Truly, truly, I say to you, unless you eat the flesh of the Son of Man and drink His blood, you have no life in yourselves.'"   (John 6:53 LSB)

However, Jesus was not even discussing the Lord's Supper. This is an evil and false doctrine. Jesus was referring to the Holy Spirit.

> The Spirit is the One who gives life; the flesh profits nothing; the words that I have spoken to you are spirit and are life.   (John 6:63 LSB)

Are we going to says that when Jesus instituted the Communion that He ate His own flesh and drank His blood?[Luk 22:19, 20] For the apostle Paul said as he quotes our Lord.

> For I received from the Lord that which I also delivered to you, that the Lord Jesus in the night in which He was betrayed took bread; and when He had given thanks, He broke it and said, **"This is My body**, which is for you; do this in remembrance of Me." In the same way He took the cup also after supper, saying, **"This cup is the new covenant** in My blood**; do this, as often as you drink it, in remembrance of Me." **For as often as you eat this bread and drink the cup, YOU <u>PROCLAIM THE LORD'S DEATH</u> until He comes**.   (1 Cor. 11:23-26)

ᶜNote: by the way, a word to hyper-dispensationalists, Paul is celebrating **THE** New Covenant note just **A** New Covenant.[2 Cor. 3:6]

Last rites:

There are no so-called last rites in the Bible. This is a lying fabrication to extract more money from gullible constituency. There is no praying for the death. Once a person dies, he/she is launched in eternity, and it is too late. There is nothing that can be done for departed dead. This is another ecclesiastical tradition and a lie right out of Hell.

If a person leaves the world without Christ Jesus as personal Lord and Savior, it is too late. They shall perish in their sin forever.

Martyrdom:

Another religious lie concocted by manmade religion is if one dies in martyrdom. No one can atone for their sins through any act of martyrdom. This is the false hope of many religions. But again, religion is manmade, and anyone relying on manmade religion shall indeed perish in their sin.

There is only one way to have our sins removed and be cleansed from sin. This is through a total commitment and trust in Jesus Christ as the Lord and only Redeemer. Without Jesus Christ as your personal Lord Savior, you will sure perish in your sins.

Conclusion

Hell is very real, and there is no escape from Hell for those who are without Christ Jesus as personal Lord and Savior. The Hebrews writer warns,

> For this reason we must pay much closer attention to what we have heard, so that we do not drift away *from it.* [2]For if the word spoken through angels proved unalterable, and every transgression and disobedience received a just penalty, [3]how will we escape if we neglect so great a salvation? After it was at the first spoken through the Lord, it was confirmed to us by those who heard, [4]God also testifying with them, both by signs and wonders and by various miracles and by gifts of the Holy Spirit according to His own will.   (Heb. 2:1-4)

The doctrine of universalism will only lead a person into Hell. They must repent and commit their life and completely trust Jesus as Lord and Savior or else they shall perish in their sin. Christ redemption is indeed available to everyone, but unless a person genuinely turns to Jesus as their only Savior, they shall perish in their sins.

Electionists distorted the doctrine of redemption. John Calvin is major leader of this doctrine, and so was Dr. Martin Luther who was stronger on the doctrine of election than Calvin.

The doctrine of election as espoused by such men above has brought death to Jesus' mandate,

> He told them, "This is what is written: The Messiah will suffer and rise from the dead on the third day, and repentance for the forgiveness of sins will be preached in his name to all nations, beginning at Jerusalem. You are witnesses of these things. (Luke 24:46-48 NIV)

Biblical evangelism is unfortunately nearly dead in many churches. You read me correction; biblical evangelism in the churches is nearly dead. Churches are no longer going "door to door" compelling people to come to Savior. What little evangelism being done, if any, is dribble. For the churches that do little evangelism, it is nothing more than trickle or drip of the Gospel. There is **no aggressive evangelism going out 24-7**, especially at night; and knocking on doors is completely abandoned.

The sentiment of many people on religion is all religions are the same. Yes, religions are all the same; they are manmade. Christianity is not a religion, it is a personal and vibrant relationship with the eternal God, Jesus Christ. Without a personal and vibrant relationship with Christ Jesus as Lord and Savior, everyone outside Christ shall perish in their sins.

There are no religious rites that can cleanse a person of his sin and make him a citizen of Heaven. As I already stated religion is manmade. So, religion and religious rites cannot make any person righteous and fit for Heaven.

> He saved us, not on the basis of deeds which we have done in righteousness, but according to His mercy, by the washing of regeneration and renewing by the Holy Spirit, ⁶ whom He poured out upon us richly through Jesus Christ our Savior, ⁷ so that being justified by His grace we would be made heirs according to *the* hope of eternal life. (Titus 3:5-7)

> For he hath made him [*Christ Jesus*] to be *sin*ᵈ for *us*, which *knew* no *sin*, that we should be made the *righteousness* of God in him.
>
> (2 Cor. 5:21 GNV)

> ᵈNote: no words have been changed; italic words are the updated words in ENG. The words in brackets "[ ]" are for clarity.

108

CHAPTER 11

Errors to enter Heaven's Gate, escaping Hell

SECTION 2:
Good works to Denial of Hell

Memory verse

The Lord is not slow about His promise, as some count slowness, but is patient toward you, not wishing for any to perish but for all to come to repentance.   (2 Peter 3:9)

Introduction

One of the arguments against many people going Hell is, "I do not believe a loving God will send anyone to Hell." As one Fundamentalist Pastor said (but was poverty stricken in biblical theology), "Oh, all the attributes of God are the same." Little did he know or comprehend that the "*holiness* and *righteousness*" of God are the Lord's highest attributes. It is from God's **holiness** and **righteousness** all other attributes flow.

So, while the Lord is infinitely loving, He will not violate His **holiness** and **righteousness**. Therefore, sins and wickedness will be judged. Those in Christ will not be judged because sin was judged at the cross for every genuine believer in Christ. For all those in Christ, there is no condemnation.[John 5:24; Rom. 8:1] Those **not** in Christ will be judged and sent to an eternal Hell without mercy.

Please listen friend, sin shall be judged. There are two elements in the judgment of God for unregenerate humanity. The Lord will judge the transgressors against His established standard, which include evil angels and unregenerate wicked humanity. Second, all in Adam shall die in their sin.

> For as in Adam all die, even so in Christ shall all be made alive.
>
> (1 Cor. 15:22 KJV)

Nowadays, there are brazen ministers of the Gospel blatantly setting themselves up as the final authority. I mean their authority overrides the inherent and innate authority of Scripture. They simply reject the authority of the Bible. Like the liberals who reject the authority of Scripture, these counterfeit ministers of the Gospel establish themselves as final authority. They have overthrown the authority the Written Word of God. They have set themselves as the final authority of the things of God.

Some of these who reject the authority of the Bible have mega churches, and they are rolling in dough ($). These are not "Name it and claim it" preachers. These are men and women void of godliness. There is no biblical repentance among them. Repentance is absent in their preaching and teaching. These people are teachers of "the Self-help," *motivational speakers* and not preachers of the Gospel. They reject the Bible and all its authority for morality and standard for godliness. These false teachers are so inflated they are the ultimate supreme authority for morality and practice. In so doing, such counterfeit workers set themselves on a collision course for the judgment of God for Hell.

The philosophy being espoused today is "Pluralism." There is no one standard in *Pluralism*. There are no absolutes. Everything is reality and constantly changing. Pluralism adamantly rejects the sovereign authority of the Bible. Those espousing Pluralism and other similar philosophies will bow their knee to Jesus Christ who is indeed the Absolute Sovereign One over all creation, [Phi.2:9-11]. Listen carefully, anyone that rejects the Bible and its authority shall realize the Lord is in control. Yes, the Word of God shall indeed have the last word.

> "I have come to cast fire upon the earth; and how I wish it were already kindled!"
>
> (Luke 12:49)

E. Sufficient good works

There is the notion by many religious people that as long as you maintain sufficient good works, then this will get you into Heaven. This is like a "credit and debit" system. If your good works outweigh your bad works, you made it. Well, who set the standard? The Lord and His Word has set the standard and not depraved humanity.

You would be surprised at some of the well-meaning International Evangelists that espouse this false doctrine. The Bible is very clear,

> For all have sinned, and come short of the glory of God.
>
> (Rom. 3:23 KJV)

> [10] As it is written, There is none righteous, no not one. [11] There is none that *understands*[a]: there is none that *seeks* God. [12] They *have* all gone out of the way: they *have* been made altogether *unprofitable*[b]: there is none that doeth good, no not one.   (Rom. 3:10-12 GNV)

> [a]Note: no words are change in GNV, only the spelling is updated.

> [b]The GK for "*unprofitable*" is "*achreioo*." An excellent translation still today. Also, the word means "*to make useless*," but I would not use "*worthless*" as used by the NIV, NET, ESV, or NRS. Christ did not die for worthless people, [Psa. 116:15].

Like Cain, who killed his brother out of jealousy; his brother Abel's works were more righteous than Cain.[1 John 3:12] Why were Abel's works more righteous? Abel brought the proper animal sacrifice for sin. Cain did not follow the standard God had established. Men and women are refusing to follow God's standard, and they are seeking to establish their own standard.[Rom. 10:3, 4]

Why is mankind seeking to establish his own righteousness before God rather than the standard determined by God in His Word, the Bible? First, mankind is ignorant of the Lord's established standard for righteousness. As noted above, Paul's statement about many Jews on this issue fit most religious people of the world.

> For, being ignorant of the righteousness of God, and seeking to establish their own, they did not submit to God's righteousness. (Rom. 10:3 ESV)

Second, humankind is seeking "a *god*" in which he has *conceived* or *manufactured* in his futile and depraved mind. Like in Hinduism that boasts of having three million *gods* and *goddesses*, man has imagined a *god* of his own making from his wicked mind.

Third, all of mankind is under the sway and influence of the world and evil forces that blind him/her from the Gospel of the Grace of God in Christ Jesus the Lord.[2 Cor. 4:3,4; Eph. 2:1-3] The Bible declares,

111

> For Christ is the end of the law for righteousness to everyone who believes. (Rom. 10:4 ESV)

The Bible is very clear,

> [16]Yet we know that a person is not justified [declared righteous]c by works of the law but [declared righteous] through faith in Jesus Christ, so we also have believed in Christ Jesus, in order to be justified [declared righteous] by faith in Christ and not by works of the law, because by works of the law no one will be justified.

> [20]I have been crucified with Christ. It is no longer I who live, but Christ who lives in me. And the life I now live in the flesh I live by faith in the Son of God, who loved me and gave himself for me. [21]I do not nullify the grace of God, for if righteousness were through the law, then Christ died for no purpose. (Gal. 2:16, 20, 21 ESV)

> cNote: "*righteous*" the same word in ENG "*justified*," GK *dikaioo*. That is, the one that is "justified" is the person "*declared righteous*" by God.

The point here is that we can only be justified or made righteous through the genuine saving faith in Christ and His work on Calvary because He bore our sins on the cross. The Lord imputes the righteousness of God to every person in Christ, [2 Cor. 5:21; Phi.3:9; 1 Peter 2:24]. No one is declared righteous by God works.

F. Sincerity is sufficient

There are others who imagine "sincerity is sufficient" to get anyone into Heaven. Let me tell you my friend, *the road that leads into Hell is paved with sincerity*. Meaning that sincerity will not get anyone into Heaven, but *sincerity will certainly put a person into Hell*. Remember: the Lord set the standard; we do not set the standard for Heaven.
Proverbs declares,

> There is a way *which seems* right to a man *and* appears straight before him, But its end is the way of death. (Prov. 14:12 AMP)

This is like the false teaching that "*it feels right; so, it is right.*" Feeling is the inner-emotion of the carnal or depraved mankind. The feelings, instinct, or intuition is governed by natural man or the old nature. Feeling does not come through new man, which is the Spirit of God.

Nowadays, travel through any large city in the world based upon intuition (especially at night) you might end up dead or nearly dead. The world is filled with unimaginable evil and unparalleled wickedness everywhere. There seems to be little restraint and law enforcement appears as though it is at a standstill. In addition, many people are *hopped-up-on* drugs, and such people have little restraint because they are given over to the stimulus. This means people may do almost anything while under the influence of the stimulus.

Sincerity is the philosophy of fools. As Solomon said,

> Do you see a person wise in their own eyes? There is more hope for a fool than for them. (Prov. 26:12 NIV)

Again in the beginning of Proverbs, Solomon said well,

> Let the wise also hear and gain in learning, and the discerning acquire skill, ⁶to understand a proverb and a figure [*figure of speech*], the words of the wise and their riddles. ⁷The fear of the LORD is the beginning of knowledge; fools despise wisdom and instruction. (Prov. 1:5-7 NRS)

A fool will not receive instruction or correction and neither will the arrogant. The arrogant is too righteous in his own eyes. Many people are too obstinate to hear correction.

> Pride *goes* before destruction, and *a* high *minded* [arrogance] before the fall. (Prov. 16:18 GNV)

The teaching that *sincerity is sufficient* is similar to *Pluralism*. In other words, do whatever you want since sincerity is paving the way. However, friend, all roads do not lead to Rome, and neither do all roads lead to Heaven. Whether anyone believes the Bible or not, this does not change anything before God who shall judge the world. The Lord shall indeed judge the world by His standard and Word. God's Word stands firmly established by the Holy Spirit. God's Word stands forever and ever.

David said in psalm 119,

> Your *Word* is forever, LORD; it is firmly established in heaven.
> (Psalm 119:89 ISV)

> A voice says, "Call out." Then he answered, "What shall I call out?" All flesh is grass, and all its loveliness is like the flower of the field. ⁷ The grass withers, the flower fades, When the breath of the LORD blows upon it; Surely the people are grass. ⁸ The grass withers, the flower fades, But the word of our God stands forever. (Isa. 40:6-8)

> Think not that I am come to destroy the law, or the prophets: I am not come to destroy, but to fulfil. For verily I say unto you, Till heaven and

> earth pass, one jot or one tittle shall in no wise pass from the law, till all
> be fulfilled.   (Matt. 5:17, 18 KJV)

Anyone building their life on sincerity, and especially without Christ Jesus as Savior, is in for a rude awaking.

A final word to those who base life on sincerity; Solomon said,

> Trust in the LORD with all your heart, And lean not on your own understanding; [6]In all your ways acknowledge Him, And He shall direct your paths. [7]Do not be wise in your own eyes; Fear the LORD and depart from evil.   (Prov. 3:5-7 NKJ)

G. Canned confession

What is "canned confession?" This is a person that may have gone through what some have called, "*the sinner's prayer*." This is where a person confesses himself as a sinner and he acknowledges he is unable to save himself before God. He acknowledges the Gospel, and he confesses to receive Jesus Christ as Lord and Savior.

So far so good? Well, yes, no, and maybe! This is a good start if the person making such confession, continues *fervently in prayer in his life*. He is also *faithfully attending* a sound Bible church. His confession may be a sound confession if he is now *confessing Christ* openly to others and declaring he has personally trusted in Christ as his Redeemer. In addition, he begins *reading e.g., the Gospel of John* and continues reading through Romans and the rest of the epistles. Most importantly, he is being *followed up* by a strong Fundamental and Bible teaching church.

Let me give you another scenario of a "canned confession." Here a person meets a person on the street, a bus, or even let us say that they meet in restaurant. A person shares the Gospel or gives a Gospel tract to the person after their confession of faith. The person takes the tract and reads it, and he then makes a confession of faith, a *canned confession*. Unfortunately, the person who gave him the tract, tell the person unwisely, that due to his *canned confession of faith* he is now "*saved*!" (Yet, the person who allegedly led him to *confession of faith* really **does not** know if the person actually got regenerated.) For instance, the person's *confession of faith* may not have genuinely received Jesus as Lord and Savior. He went through form without substance. It was a sham! Is he saved?

Well, what are the facts following the "canned confession?" He says he is saved because the person witnessing to him told him he is saved. (Red flag!)

However, this person that made the confession he _never_ _bother to pray ever._ (Red flag!) He does _not attend church,_ but he thinks he is saved because he was told by the evangelist that he is saved. Listen, God's Spirit will testify with our spirit if we are truly saved.[Rom. 8:16]

In addition, this same person has _never confessed Christ_ as his personal Lord and Savior even though he professes to believe in his heart. (Red flag!) He does not read the Bible, and he has no plans to a buy Bible since he is saved. (Red flag.) He is relying on what the man who witnessed to him told him that he was saved because he _allegedly_ repeated "the _Sinner's Prayer._" The man is not relying on God's Word or his faith in Christ! There is no further connection with the person who gave him the tract, and he has no connection to any sound Evangelical church. Worse of all, **there is no follow up** by a church. (Red flag!)

What is missing here? There is **no fruit** in his life. That is, there is **no evidence** of the person's spiritual walk or lifestyle in Christ. There is **no difference in his life** since his "canned confession" in Christ. No one can genuinely confess that he repented and received the risen and glorified Christ Jesus but remain unchanged! The genuine confession of faith in Christ **will be exhibited** with a definite **spiritual transformation** because the Spirit of the living God is in him. (If he/she is genuinely saved and indwelt by Holy Spirit but continues to live wickedly, then, God will kill them and take them to Heaven.) If there is no change, it is likely his "canned confession" is a **dud**; his confession professed was not a genuine possession by Spirit of God.

The Bible says for those who truly know Christ the Lord-

> For Christ's love compels [engulfs] us, because we are convinced that one died for all, and therefore all [believers] died. [15]And he [Christ] died for all [believers], that those [believers] who live should no longer live for themselves but for him [Christ] who died for them and was raised again. [16]So from now on we regard no one from a worldly point of view. Though we once regarded Christ in this way, we do so no longer. [17]Therefore, if anyone is [truly] in Christ, the new creation has come: The old has gone, the new is here! (2 Cor. 5:14-17 NIV)

Yes, Christ Jesus the Lord died for all mankind. However, the context 2 Corinthians 5 and Christ's sacrifice for sin is dealing particularly with the genuine believer. Paul does not mean the world in this specific context.

So, with anyone's confession of faith, we may rightly ask:

"Where is the fruit of regeneration?"

"What evidence is there that demonstrates the genuineness of their confession of faith in Christ?" Not what he says but what changed in his life?

Genuine faith in Jesus Christ will be evident. Genuine faith is demonstrated with action. This is the point of Hebrews 11. By the same token, James says,

> In the same way, faith by itself, if it is not accompanied by action[d], is dead. (James 2:17 NIV)

> [d]Note: GK word is "*ergon*." *Ergon* means *deeds* or *works*, but connotative meaning is- *it is evident with **action***. Furthermore, we are not saved by works,[Eph. 2:8-10] but if one has genuine faith in Christ, it will be evident in their walk of faith by good works or actions.[Eph. 2:8-10]

H. Denial of Hell

The denial of Hell, Heaven, or the existence of God does not change anything. The Lord God and His Heaven and Hell exist whether a person believes it or not. Anyone denying Hell, Heaven, or God is in for a very *rude awakening*. The person will stand before the Lord for judgment, and they shall be *terror stricken*. Everyone from the most arrogant atheist to the most ignorant fool will be terror stricken.

The apostle John knows what *terror stricken* means when he came into the very presence of the risen and glorified the Lord Jesus Christ:

> [13]And in the middle of the lampstands [e.g., *the churches*] *I saw* one like a son of man, clothed in a robe reaching to the feet, and girded across His chest with a golden sash. [14]His head and His hair were white like white wool, like snow; and His eyes were like a flame of fire. [15]His feet *were* like burnished [*highly polished*] bronze, when it has been made to glow in a furnace, and His voice *was* like the sound of many waters [*thundering loud*]. [16]In His right hand He held seven stars [*Pastors*], and out of His mouth came a sharp two-edged sword; and His face was like the sun shining in its strength [*blinding brightness*]. [17]**When I saw Him, I fell at His feet like a dead man**. And He placed His right hand on me, saying, "Do not be afraid; I am the first and the last, [18] and the living One; and I was dead, and behold, I am alive forevermore, and I have the keys of death and of Hades[e]. (Rev. 1:13-18)

ᵉNote: KJV uses the word "hell," but the GK word is literally "hades." Hades will be cast into the Lake of Fire, which is Hell.[Rev. 20:14] The meaning is likely referring to the "*grave*."

Keep in mind concerning the redeemed as the apostle Peter says,

> And if the righteous are barely saved, what will become of the ungodly and sinners? (1 Peter 4:18 NET)

The unregenerate standing before the Great White Throne Judgment shall be *terror stricken* beyond comprehension. The unbeliever shall know what it means to be *speechless*. *Petrifying fear* [the feeling of being *stone-dead*] and cannot describe the overwhelming dread that will come over them.

My friend as we noted earlier, the seraphim angels that are most holy and absolutely without any sin. Yet, the seraphim with two wings cover the face, with two wings cover the feet, and with two wings fly crying out loud: 'Holy, Holy, Holy is the Lord Almighty.' Even the whole temple shook. What then shall it be like for sinful and wicked unregenerate to stand in the presence of a Holy God? Awesome and dreadful is the Lord our God. Hallelujah!

Unbelievable, but, many professing Christian **do not fear the LORD**. Many professing saints walk into worship service like walking into a ball game. There is no evidence of reverence, awe, adoration, and certainly no fear. People milling around and talking or sipping their latte or coffee.

Little do people realize that the King is present (the Lord is present in church service), and yes, so are His awesome holy angels present with Him. It is not surprising that the unregenerate follow the same example or pattern and attitude of the professing believers. The unbelievers emulate what they see the professing Christian leaders and believers do.

All the above will drastically change in the Lord's physical presence when we see Him in all His glory as the apostle John saw Jesus in Heaven. The professing believers today are too glib in their attitude, actions, and worship. The saints' glib attitude has helped falter and generate unregenerate's attitude towards the Lord and worship.

Let me warn those who scoff and mock the living God. Wake up my friend before the door into eternity opens and there is no turning back. I know the Lord in His infinite mercy and grace has sought to illuminate and warn you. Do not harden your heart against the wooing and convicting power of the blessed Holy Spirit. God is only trying reach you.

> Behold, now *is* the accepted time; behold, now *is* the day of salvation. (2 Cor. 6:2b NKJ)

Conclusion

Friend, Hell is real, and Hell is no joke. No; you shall not have a lot of company in Hell. You shall be all alone in Hell. It shall be utter pitch-darkness. (Darker than being lowered in a very deep coal mine where there is no light). You will experience infinite and endless suffering in Hell. You will be totally consumed with bitterness, untold rage, and anger. You will still have the old nature in Hell.

The Lord God offers you love, forgiveness, peace, and endless fellowship, even in the "**here and now** as well throughout eternity in Christ." However, I warn you do not be foolish and scorn and mock God's Word. Do not mock He grace of redemption out of Hell. At death, it is too late.[Heb. 9:27] Now the day of reckoning is coming! There is no retrieve or appeal. You have sealed your own fate forever and ever.

The Lord Jesus warns,

> I said, therefore, to you, that you will die in your sins, for if you may not believe that **I AM**, you will die in your sins."   (John 8:24 LSV)

CHAPTER 12

The Door into Utter-Darkness and Separation

Memory verse

Then said the king to the servants, Bind him hand and foot, and take him away, and cast *him* into outer darkness; there shall be weeping and gnashing of teeth. (Matt. 22:13 KJV)

Introduction

The memory verse is from a parable of a great King that gave a banquet. Many of those invited either ignored or dismissed the special occasion to the King's banquet. (The parable refers to many Jews that did not believe the Gospel.) The invitation is the Gospel, receiving Jesus as Lord and Savior, which is open to everyone.

Apparently, one individual, *snubbed* the invitation certificate, but he just arrogantly and boldly entered the King's banquet without the free certificate and entering the banquet on his own accord. So, he *brushed off* and *spurned* the free invitation certificate, which included free attire (free amenities) provided at the King's expense. Snubbing the King's free certified invitation and walking into the King's banquet without a certification of a royal banquet was a very serious and grave offense. This is especial true when the King provided free preparation, *"even pampered bathing,"* and royal attire for the banquet. Ignoring the royal attire and the King's amenities was even a greater offense. The ultimate offense was brazenly walking into a royal banquet with street clothes and ignoring the royal protocol and security were very grievous offense.

The man showed mockery and arrogant disrespect for a very high wedding for the King's son. The action of busting into a national or international royal banquet of a powerful King which had very tight and stringent security meant the sentence of death. The person could have accepted the invitation and followed the King's draconian law, security, and protocol and all would have been fine.

In the same way, the invitation to Heaven is open to all, but ignoring Jesus Christ and the Gospel (free to all) is a dreadful and horrific infinite offense to the Lord and His holy and righteous standard. This is a very grave insult to the Spirit of God. Rejecting salvation through the Lord Jesus, he is actually condemning himself to Hell forever and ever.

> "He who believes in Him is not condemned; but he who does not believe **is condemned already,** because he has not believed in the name of the only begotten Son of God." (John 3:18 NKJ)

> "He who believes in the Son has everlasting life; and he who **does not believe the Son shall not see life,** but **the wrath of God abides on him.**" (John3:36 NKJ)

The meaning implied is that Jesus Christ the Lord is the only means into Heaven. There is no other way into Heaven.

> Neither is there salvation in any other: for there is none other name under heaven given among men, whereby we must be saved.
>
> (Acts 4:12 KJV)

> [28]A man who disregards Moses' law dies without compassion on the word of two or three witnesses. [29]How much worse punishment do you think he will be judged worthy of who has trodden *underfoot* the Son of God, and has counted the blood of the [*New*] *Covenant* with which he was sanctified an unholy thing, and has insulted the Spirit of grace? [30]For we know him who said, "Vengeance belongs to me. I will repay," says the Lord. Again, "The Lord will judge his people." [31]It is a fearful thing to fall into the hands of the living God. (Heb. 10:28-31 WEB)

Listen my friend, Hebrews' warning is not just to unbelievers but also believers. Friend, let us be so ever careful not show contempt for the shed blood and death of Christ. I am sorry to say and even fearful that many are show contempt for Jesus Christ in absolute ignorance to His sacrifice on Calvary.

So, the parable in Matt. 22 reflects a scorning warning to everyone reject-ing Jesus Christ's loving offer of eternal salvation through Him. Jesus is the only One that provides the certified invitation by the Spirit of the living God into Heaven. There is no other way into Heaven except through Jesus Christ. If anyone tries to enter Heaven any other way except by repenting and genuinely committing their life to Jesus as Sovereign Lord and only Redeemer, they are committing spiritual suicide. They will certainly be cast into Hell.

> Then said the king to the servants, Bind him hand and foot, and take
> him away, and cast *him* into outer darkness; there shall be weeping and
> gnashing of teeth. (Matt. 22:13 KJV)

Therefore, anyone foolish enough to disregard the biblical protocol (refus-ing Jesus Christ as Lord and Savior) shall be sent into an eternal Hell, 'outer darkness. There shall be weeping and gnashing of teeth.'[Matt. 22:13]

Listen friend, there is no retrieve from Hell. Hell is very, very real. Hell is forever and ever. Again, Hebrews dreadfully warns us:

> Anyone who rejected the law of Moses died without mercy on the
> testimony of two or three witnesses. [29]How much more severely do you
> think someone deserves to be punished who has trampled the Son of
> God underfoot, who has treated as an unholy thing the blood of the
> covenant that sanctified them, and who has insulted the Spirit of grace?
> [30]For we know him who said, "It is mine to avenge; I will repay," and
> again, "The Lord will judge his people." [31]It is a dreadful thing to fall
> into the hands of the living God. (Heb. 10:28-31 NIV)

Friend, I am warning you, there is no escape from Hell once you enter the door into eternity without Christ as Savior. Hell is forever and ever. Believe and receive Jesus as Sovereign Lord and only Redeemer, or else, you shall surely perish in your sins in Hell.

A. Total Darkness forever

In the previous chapter, I alluded to total darkness of Hell (*utterly pitch-darkness*). Unfortunately, many teachers of the Bible with deficient or defec-tive knowledge in *biblical and systematic theology* will come up short. The Bible is no ordinary book. The Bible was written and given to us by the Spirit of the eternal God. Without wooing, enlightenment and illumination of the Spirit of God, the natural man is helpless in understanding God word.

> But the natural [unbelieving] man does not accept the things [the teachings and revelations] of the Spirit of God, for they are foolishness [absurd and illogical] to him; and he is incapable of understanding them, because they are spiritually discerned *and* appreciated, [and he is unqualified to judge spiritual matters]. (1 Cor. 2:14 AMP)

In addition, many seriously err with *deficiency in the Scriptural teaching.* Many err simply because they only study doctrine, but they are not in *avid* and *zealous* study and reading faithfully and regularly through all the Bible. (They study doctrine of men and espoused by their established tradition). Sadly, I am telling you many are spiritually bankrupt. They have no hunger or thrust to zealously systemically, faithfully, and regularly reading and studying **all of God's Word, OT and NT**.

Let us consider the rich man in [Luke 16]. The rich man was originally named "Dives" in the KJV, a literal transliteration from the Latin Vulgate into the original KJV 1611 edition. Later, the KJV changed to the GK meaning, "rich man." *Dives* (the rich man) was in Hades awaiting judgment. He was **not** in Hell. Hell is actually the Lake of Fire or also referred to as the eternal fire.[Matt. 18:8; 25:41; Jude 1:7] Revelation reveals that *death and hades are cast into Hell.*[Rev. 20:14]

In addition, Jesus refers to the abode of the righteous as "Abraham's bosom," which is likely a unique phrase in HEB referring to Heaven. No one can see anyone in Heaven. In the same way, no one can see others on earth anyone in Heaven or in Hell. Neither can one of those who are in Hades or Hell see anyone. False teachers, naïve, gullible, credulous, the delusional, and all liars have alleged that they have gone to Heaven and returned. Listen, no one has gone Heaven or Hell and returned to tell us about it. and John are the only one returned from Heaven. There is no one who has entered Hell and came back to tell about. Such alleged claims by people are either liars of the worst sort or self-deluded. Hades is a holding place for the unregenerate until the judgment. Again, the Bible says of hades,

> Then Death and Hades[a][1] were cast into the lake of fire. This is the second death. (Rev. 20:14 NKJ)

> [a]Note: The KJV uses the word "Hell," but the GK word is literally "*hades*," which is equivalent to the HEB "*sheol*." (See note # 1)

Some hyper-dispensationalists falsely teach that "hades" is the abode of the *righteous* and *unrighteous* before the resurrection of Jesus Christ. Such teachers allege that there are two separate and distinct compartments in Hades: Abraham's bosom and the above of the unsaved. This is a very grievous and notorious error. There is no basis for such insertion. There are **not** two compartments in Hades. This is a serious defect by hyper-dispensationalists. The redeemed are immediately taken to Heaven at death. **Do not believe their error!**

Still others such as the cults like the Seventh Day Adventists and other cults allege everyone remains dead like a dead animal at death. Hence, the cults allege there is no existence of life after death. At death everyone, the saved and unsaved, have vanished, they are gone. There is no existence once a person has died according to such cults. At death, everyone is completely erased from life. What biblical illiteracy, spiritual blindness, and being brain-dead!

The cults call their evil doctrine, "soul sleep," but such name by cult is misleading and a *bold-faced lie*. Actually, the cults mean that the soul refers the *breath* of life, and spirit means *being alive*. So, at death, the person is completely disintegrated. They are no longer in existence after death until the resurrection according to such depraved cults.

So, at death, humans only exist in the *memory of God* according such cults. By the memory of God, the Lord will call everyone back into existence again for judgment. Then cults maintain that the condemned (evil angels and unregenerate) are obliterated or annihilated in Hell or Lake of Fire, and they no longer exist. They are gone forever. They are erased from life forever. There is no suffering in Hell forever according to such cults.

However, to the contrary, the Bible is abundantly clear, everyone is very much alive in their souls the moment they die. The saved are in Heaven in their souls, but the unsaved await the judgment in "hades." Jesus rebuked the Sadducees who did not believe in the afterlife. Sadducees were like the liberal and cults today. Our Lord said,

> [29]Jesus answered them, "You are **deceived**, because you **don't know** the **scriptures** or the **power of God**. [30]For in the resurrection they neither marry nor are given in marriage, but are like angels in heaven. [31]Now as for the resurrection of the dead, have you not read what was spoken to you by God, [32]**'I am the God of Abraham, the God of Isaac, and the God of Jacob'**? He is not the God of the dead but [*the God*] of the living!" (Matt. 22:29-33 NET)

The fact Enoch and Elijah ascended to Heaven without dying ought to remove such error by hyper-dispensationalists on their erroneous doctrine of hades. The cults are blinded by Satan, and even if the truth were plainly declared to them by the angel Gabriel, they would not believe it.

Furthermore, Jesus explicitly and emphatically declared He saw Abraham after his death (an inference Christ the Lord saw Abraham in Heaven).

> [56]"Your father Abraham rejoiced to see My day, and he saw *it* and was glad." [57]So the Jews said to Him, "You are not yet fifty years old, and have You seen Abraham?" [58]Jesus said to them, "Truly, truly, I say to you, before Abraham was born, **I AM**." (John 8:56-58)

The apostle Paul plainly taught that upon save's death that the redeemed ascend to Heaven.[Phi. 1:21-23; 2 Cor. 5:8] Jesus said to the thief on the cross that believed in Him,

> Then he said to Jesus, "Lord, remember me when You come into Your kingdom." And Jesus said to him, "Assuredly, I say to you, today you will be with Me in Paradise." (Luke 23:42, 43 NKJ)

The Bible describes the terror of Hell

The Geneva Bible of 1599 translates Hell in Jude this way,

> "— they are *wandering stars*[b], to *whom* is *reserved* the **blackness of darkness** forever." (Jude 1:13b GNV)

> [b]Note: no words have been changed; only the words in in italics have been updated. Geneva Bible still is an excellent translation today.

Jude describes Hell as absolutely **utter-darkness**, or **totally void of any light**. This is a portrait of anyone in Hell. In Hell, a person is not able to even see even his hand in front of him.

Jesus said concerning the unbelievers,

> And cast ye the unprofitable servant into outer darkness: there shall be weeping and gnashing of teeth. (Matt. 25:30 KJV)

Even after the thousand-year reign of Christ and the Great White Throne Judgment, we read this statement concerning the evil angels and unsaved,

> "But for the cowardly and unbelieving and abominable and murderers and immoral persons and sorcerers and idolaters and all liars, their part *will be* in the lake that burns with fire and brimstone, which is the second death." (Rev. 21:8)

So, even in the new creation after New Heavens, New Jerusalem, and New Earth, we continue to read this concerning all those outside Christ's redemption,

Outside are the dogs and the sorcerers and the immoral persons and the murderers and the idolaters, and everyone who loves and practices lying.   (Rev. 22:15)

No one is annihilated, eradicated, or exterminated in Hell. Suffering in Hell is forever and ever without Christ Jesus as Lord and Savior.

*Special note on the false teaching of "**outer darkness**."*

In particularly, the text in Matt. 25:30 has been abused and very depraved and wicked teaching has emerged by some teachers of the Bible. This is a parable from.[Matt. 25:14-30] This ought to serve as a serious warning to anyone attempting to build a doctrine from a parable. Do not every use a parable to teach biblical doctrine. Parables are given as illustration and not to build some doctrine. Here is the text:

[14]"For *it is* just like a man *about* to go on a journey, *who* called his own slaves and entrusted his possessions to them. [15]To one he gave five talents, to another, two, and to another, one, each according to his own ability; and he went on his journey. [16]The one who had received the five talents immediately went and did business with them, and earned five more *talents.* [17]In the same way the one who *had received* the two *talents* earned two more. [18]But he who received the one *talent* went away and dug *a hole in the* ground, and hid his master's money."

(vv 14-18)

[19]"Now after a long time the master of those slaves came and settled accounts with them. [20]The one who had received the five talents came up and brought five more talents, saying, 'Master, you entrusted five talents to me. See, I have earned five more talents.' [21]His master said to him, 'Well done, good and faithful slave. You were faithful with a few things, I will put you in charge of many things; enter the joy of your master.'   (vv 19-21)

[22]"Also the one who *had received* the two talents came up and said, 'Master, you entrusted two talents to me. See, I have earned two more talents.' [23]His master said to him, 'Well done, good and faithful slave. You were faithful with a few things, I will put you in charge of many things; enter the joy of your master.'   (vv 22, 23)

[24]"Now the one who had received the one talent also came up and said, 'Master, I knew you to be a hard man, reaping where you did not sow,

and gathering where you did not scatter *seed.* [25]And I was afraid, so I went away and hid your talent in the ground. See, you *still* have what is yours.' [26]But his master answered and said to him, 'You worthless, lazy slave! Did you know that I reap where I did not sow, and gather where I did not scatter *seed?* [27]Then you ought to have put my money in the bank, and on my arrival I would have received my *money* back with interest. [28]Therefore: take the talent away from him, and give it to the one who has the ten talents.'"   (vv 24-28)

[29]"For to everyone who has, *more* shall be given, and he will have an abundance; but from the one who does not have, even what he does have shall be taken away. [30]And throw the worthless slave into the outer darkness; in that place there will be weeping and gnashing of teeth. [vv 29, 30] (Matt. 25:14-30)

Note the key sentence,

> `And cast the unprofitable servant into the **outer darkness**. There will
> be weeping and gnashing of teeth.'   (Matt. 25:30 NKJ)

The phrase *'outer darkness'* is refers to hell. *'Outer darkness'* is a phrase meaning Hell, **for the unbeliever**; it is **never** used of believers.(See Matt. 13:28, 38, 50; 24: 51; 2 Peter 2:17; Jude 1:13.)

But the sons of the kingdom [unbelieving Jews] will be cast out into outer darkness. There will be weeping and gnashing of teeth." Mat. 8:12 Then said the king to the servants, Bind him hand and foot, and take him away, and cast *him* into outer darkness [unbelieving Jews]; there shall be weeping and gnashing of teeth. Mat. 22:13 `And cast the unprofitable servant [unbelieving Jews] into the outer darkness. There will be weeping and gnashing of teeth.' Mat. 25:30	[40]Therefore as the tares are gathered and burned in the fire, so it will be at the end of this age. [41]The Son of Man will send out His angels, and they will gather out of His kingdom all things that offend [unbelieving], and those who practice lawlessness, [42]and will cast them into the furnace of fire. There will be wailing and gnashing of teeth. [43]Then the righteous [believing] will shine forth as the sun in the kingdom of their Father. He who has ears to hear, let him hear! Mat. 13:40-43

Jesus is giving this parable those are unsaved. When studying a parable, you should only look for the simple truth being taught. Never expand or probe a parable to examined for detail. Parable is just laying down a *contrasts* or *comparison* between opposites. The simple truth is contrasting those who are **redeemed** and those who only had profession of faith but remain **unregenerated**.

The contrast is between unbelieving Jewish leaders and genuine Jewish believers. The unbelievers are cast in "**outer darkness**." **Outer darkness** is where *"weeping and gnashing of teeth."* **Outer darkness** is also reserved for the devil and other evil angels. **Outer darkness** is the abode of all unregenerate or unbelievers.[Matt. 25:41, 46] Pay attention: **outer darkness** is never use in reference to genuine believer!

The KJV translation *"unprofitable"* [GK *achreios*] or *"unworthy"* or *"useless"* is preferred. The translation of *"worthless"* is not the meaning. No person is worthless since man is created in the image or likeness of God.[Gen.1:26] The *"useless"* are those without the indwelling Holy Spirit, the unregenerate. Such people prove that they are unsaved by not exhibiting any fruit of the Holy Spirit which is only produced by the Holy Spirit. This is very evident of counterfeit ministers. Counterfeit ministers are false teachers. Jesus is **not** addressing the general people in this parable. This is more applicable to counterfeit Pastors or false preachers or false teachers. This is referring to the general believers. The unregenerate are incapable of producing genuine spiritual fruit for God since it is the Spirit from above that must actually produce the fruit.

Everyone, when he is saved, is **saved by grace**. No one is ever saved by religious works.[Rom. 11:6; Eph. 2:8-10; Titus 3:3-7] *Outer darkness* refers to Hell, and no genuine believer will lose his salvation.[John 6:37-40; 10:28-30] Again, *outer darkness* refers to Hell, the abode of the unregenerate outside Christ's redemption.

The word "talent" (GK *talanton*) is a very, very large sum of money. NAS suggest equaling "Just one talent was worth about fifteen years' wages of a laborer." Wow! The Bible word talent does **not** mean abilities or skills. In the parable, these three were apparently *financial advisers* or *financial consultants* for a king's treasures and overall wealth.[Matt. 25:14-30] The king provides the financial backing to invest the king's treasury or the king's revenue.

Anyone using the parable to manipulate or coerce others into giving money will be severely judged by our Lord Himself.[James 3:1] Mark my words! Our Lord sternly warns,

> But I say unto you, That every idle word that men shall speak, they shall
> give account thereof in the day of judgment.　　　(Matt. 12:36 KJV)

B. Complete separation from everyone

As I have said, some mock God and His Hell as they imagine themselves, "Well, in Hell, I will have a lot of company. Ha, ha!" In Hell, it is *pitch-black* and absence or *void of any light* and all things. Each person is separated from everyone else. They are all alone. A person is completely isolated from everyone and everything. A person in Hell is totally by themselves, and they are on their own.

There is no one to comfort the unregenerate suffering in Hell. People are in solitude and completely in seclusion from others. The anguish and anxiety one must feel will be terrifying, unimaginable, and excruciating pain. Keep in mind that it is total darkness (pitch-black) in Hell. Whether or not one can hear the anguish of others in Hell, I do not know. What a horrifying and dreadful feeling it will be in Hell for the mocker of living and eternal God and His Hell.

Even the flames in Hell may not provide any light. (Yes, even the flames in Hell are unable to given light.) In Hell, there is torturing and tormenting suffering. Yet, amazingly, the unregenerate will reflect no sorrow or biblical repentance since the person is overcome and totally consumed with his/her old nature. Like *Dives* in hades in,[Luke 16:19ff] the *rich man* exhibited no remorse or any sense of godly repentance. He was still very egocentric and extremely arrogant. The rich man still viewed Lazarus as a worthless beggar. *Dives* still had a very high estimation of himself in comparison to Lazarus. In Hades and in his torment, he said to Abraham,

> — the rich man [*Dives*] also died and was buried. ²³"In Hades he lifted up his eyes, **being in torment**, and saw Abraham far away and Lazarus in his bosom. ²⁴"And he cried out and said, 'Father Abraham, have mercy on me, and **send Lazarus** so that he may **dip the tip of his finger in water** and cool off my tongue, for **I am in agony in this flame**.'

> (Luke 16:22b-24)

Please listen! In Hell, there is **no sense of regret**. There is **no remorse for sin**. There is **not even any evidence of compunction**. There is **not even any shame in living wicked and unbelieving life**. So, even in Hell the unregenerate is incapable of repentance or contrition. He is totally enraged and consumed by his raging old nature within him, and this is because he is void of the new nature which is only given by the Spirit of God.

Without the new nature, the Spirit of God within a person, the unsaved is totally engulfed with bitterness and rage.
King David has a word for those who dare to mock the Lord and His Word,

> Let your steadfast love come to me, O LORD, your salvation according to your promise; ⁴²then shall I have an answer for him who taunts me, for I trust in your word. ⁴³And take not the word of truth utterly out of my mouth, for my hope is in your rules. ⁴⁴I will keep your law

continually, forever and ever, [45]and I shall walk in a wide place, for I have sought your precepts. [46]I will also speak of your testimonies before kings and shall not be put to shame, [47]for I find my delight in your commandments, which I love.   (Psa. 119:41-47 ESV)

Some imagine that in Hell the unregenerate will repent. No! There is no godly repentance without the Holy Spirit. The natural man is incapable of changing his old nature. There is no repentance without the Holy Spirit. Repentance is the work of the Spirit of God.[John 16:7-11] The natural man can do nothing through his unregenerate nature to please God. As our Lord said as given by NET,

The Spirit is the one who gives life; human nature is of no help!

(John 6:63a NET)

Salvation is the work of God! So, the unregenerate is unable to change himself. The change must come from above by the Spirit of the living God. Hallelujah! This is why our Lord told Nicodemus,

Jesus answered him, "Very truly, I tell you, no one can see the kingdom of God without **being born from above**." [4]Nicodemus said to him, "How can anyone be born after having grown old? Can one enter a second time into the mother's womb and be born?" [5]Jesus answered, "Very truly, I tell you, no one can enter the kingdom of God without being born of water and Spirit. [6]**What is born of the flesh is flesh**, and **what is born of the Spirit is spirit**. [7]Do not be astonished that I said to you, **'You must be born from above.'**   (John 3:3-7 NRS)

Water baptism can never remove sin. Anyone teaching water baptism removes sin is a deceiving liar. Friend, the water is the Word of God.

So that He might sanctify her, **having cleansed her by the washing of water with the word**.   (Eph. 5:26)

But when the kindness of God our Savior and *His* love for mankind appeared, He saved us, not on the basis of deeds which we have done in righteousness, but according to His mercy, **by the washing of regeneration and renewing by the Holy Spirit**.   (Titus 3:4, 5)

It is possible that Jesus contrasting the natural physical birth (a woman breaking water before giving birth) and the Holy Spirit given (birth from above),

> Jesus answered, "Very truly, I tell you, no one can enter the kingdom of God without being born of water and Spirit. What is born of the flesh is flesh, and what is born of the Spirit is spirit.   (John 3:5, 6 NRS)

Nevertheless, the unregenerate cannot remain passive if he want to be genuinely saved. (This is the error of many *electionists*; they are too passive in their doctrine of genuine salvation.) He/she must **personally <u>seek</u> the Lord** and must personally **<u>trust</u> in Christ** and must personally **<u>receive</u> the Gospel**. And if the confession is genuine, then, there will begin the transformation of regeneration. Otherwise, that person or persons shall indeed die in their sin and without mercy.

> I said, therefore, to you, that you will die in your sins, for if you may not believe that I AM, you will die in your sins."   (John 8:24 LSV)

> He came to what was his own, and his own people did not accept him. **But to all who <u>RECEIVED</u> <u>HIM</u>, who <u>BELIEVED</u>** [*genuinely trust*] **<u>IN</u> <u>HIS</u> <u>NAME</u>, <u>HE</u> <u>GAVE</u> <u>POWER</u> <u>TO</u> <u>BECOME</u> <u>CHILDREN</u> <u>OF</u> <u>GOD</u>**, who were born, not of blood or of the will of the flesh or of the will of man, but of God.   (John 1:11-13 NRS)

Salvation is not based on believing the historical facts of the God. He personal must personally call upon the Lord Jesus to saved. When a person truly makes a genuine commitment and trusts Jesus as Lord and Savior, then, he passes from death into eternal life.[John 5:24]

Conclusion

Friend, it is no joke to be cast into Hell. Hell is total isolation, and it is completely and absolutely void of any light. Isaiah maybe describing Hell when he says,

> Distressed and hungry, they will roam through the land; when they are famished, they will become enraged and, looking upward, will curse their king and their God. Then they will look toward the earth and see only distress and darkness and fearful gloom, and **they will be thrust into utter darkness**.   (Isa. 8:21, 22 NIV)

> These are springs without water and mists driven by a storm, **for whom the black darkness has been reserved**.   (2 Peter 2:17)

> And cast ye the unprofitable servant **into outer darkness: there shall be weeping and gnashing of teeth**.   (Matt. 25:30 KJV)

Friend, I am trying my best to warn you. The Lord is an infinitely holy and righteous God. He will indeed not only judge the sin; listen to me, the Lord will judge every sinner that is not in Christ.

Hell was prepared for the devil and the evil angels that followed him, but everyone that **DOES NOT** genuinely repent of their sin and genuine trust in Jesus Christ will be thrusted into the Lake of Fire forever and ever. Trust in Jesus Christ as Lord and Savior right now. He will indeed save you.

> Because **if you confess with your mouth** that **JESUS IS LORD** and **believe in your heart** that God raised him from the dead, **YOU WILL BE SAVED.** [10]For **with the heart one believes** and thus has righteousness and **with the mouth one confesses and thus has salvation.** [11]For the scripture says, "Everyone who believes in him will not be put to shame." [12]For there is no distinction between the Jew and the Greek, for the same Lord is Lord of all, who richly blesses all who call on him. [13]**FOR EVERYONE WHO CALLS ON THE NAME OF THE LORD WILL BE SAVED.**   (Rom. 10:9-13 NET)

The Philippian jailer asked Paul and Silas how to be saved, and they said,

> Then he [the Philippian Jailer] called for a light, ran in, and fell down trembling before Paul and Silas. [30]And he brought them out and said, "**Sirs, what must I do to be saved?**" [31]So they said, "**BELIEVE ON THE LORD JESUS CHRIST, AND YOU WILL BE SAVED**, you and your household."   (Acts 16:29-31 NKJ)

Paul and Silas said that the promise of God is for everyone that genuinely places their trust Christ, the Lord shall truly save them and make them a citizen of Heaven today. The promise is legitimately offered and available to everyone. Each person in the family must place their trust in Jesus and receive Him today. Yes, trust and receive Jesus as your personal Lord and Savior. Jesus will save you from your sins right now.

Footnotes:

1.   The word is "Hell" in the KJV, but the GK is "hades." Hades is the equivalent for HEB word for "sheol." Friberg Analytical GK Lex. says of the word "*hades*,"

> "Hades (literally *unseen place*); (1) the place of the dead *underworld* (Acts 2.27); (2) usually in the NT as the temporary underworld prison where the souls of the ungodly await the judgment (Luke 16.23); (3) personified as following along after Death (Rev. 6.8)."

Dank's Lex. says,

"'Hades' is god of the underworld/netherworld, which is frequently associated with his name as 'house/abode of Hades'; in later Gk. the focus is frequently on Hades as locale, and in most Israelite circles the Greek term would be understood in the sense of the Heb. 'sheol'] 'abode of the dead', **Deathplace, Netherworld, Hades** Acts 2:27, 31; as opposed to heaven **Matt. 11:23;** with subdivisions for torment and blessing (approaching the standard Hellenic perception) **Luke 16:23.** In **Rev. 6:8** the netherworld is perceived as a functioning entity; cp. the extraordinary imagery **20:14.**"

2. A "talent," as noted by NAS is equal to fifteen years income for common laborer in NT times. Others maintain a talent is equal to 20 twenty years labor. So, just one talent is a very large sum of money. The GK word *talanton* for talent **does not** refer to *abilities* or *skills*. This is money that the King gave to his investors for the royal treasury as his personal stewards.

CHAPTER 13

The Door into
endless Bitterness and Anger

Memory verse

And many sleeping in the earth of dust shall awake, these to eternal life,
and these to reproach and eternal abhorrence.   (Dan. 12:2 SLT)

Introduction

I am deeply sorry for those who have rejected God's Word concerning faith in the risen and glorified Lord and Savior Jesus Christ. The Lord offered them and everyone else eternal life through Himself forever and ever in Heaven. If anyone chooses not to believe God's Word, the Bible, they shall suffer eternally for their rejection of His gracious offer.

I also say that I am more deeply saddened for those who have followed the *god* of their own manufactured depraved mind. As a result of their rejection of Christ the Lord, they are lost forever. Yes, and even more so, I have unceasing tears of sorrow for those who only have professions *of faith* in Jesus Christ, but they are without Christ as their Savior. These are people completely deceived and *absent* of genuine *possession of saving faith*. Regrettably, they missed redemption in Christ Jesus the Lord because they did not genuinely trust and receive Jesus as their personal Lord and only Savior.

Still others have been engulfed and led astray by their carnal nature, the attractions and deceptions of the world system, and even partially demonic blindness. (I say "*partially blindness*" since the devil and the evil angels can never keep anyone from the power of the Gospel of Christ.) Friend, I warn you, what the Scripture warns us below is no laughing matter. As the apostle Paul declares,

> And you were dead in the trespasses and sins ²in which you once walked, **following the course of this world, following the prince** of the power of the air, **the spirit that is now at work in the sons of disobedience**— ³among whom we all once lived in the passions of our flesh, carrying out the **desires of the body** and **the mind**, and were **by nature children of wrath**, like the rest of mankind. (Eph. 2:1-3 ESV)

The Bible is very clear that the Lord does not want any person to perish in their sin. The Lord would rather people should repent and trust and receive Jesus as the Lord and the only Redeemer.

> The Lord is not slack concerning his promise, as some men count slackness; but is longsuffering to us-ward, **not willing that any should perish, but** that **all should come to repentance**.   (2 Peter 3:9 KJV)

> I urge, then, first of all, that <u>petitions</u>, <u>prayers</u>, <u>intercession</u> and <u>thanksgiving</u> be **made for ALL PEOPLE**— ²for kings and all those in authority, that we may live peaceful and quiet lives in all godliness and holiness. ³**This is good, and pleases God** our Savior, ⁴**who WANTS ALL PEOPLE TO BE SAVED** and **TO COME TO A KNOWLEDGE OF THE TRUTH**. ⁵For there is one God and one mediator between God and mankind, the man Christ Jesus,   (1 Tim. 2:1-5 NIV)

> For it is for this we labor and strive, because we have fixed our **hope on the living God**, who **is THE SAVIOR OF ALL MEN**, especially of believers.   (1 Tim. 4:10)

Even as the Lord Jesus told Nicodemus,

> "For **GOD SO LOVED THE WORLD**, that he gave his only Son, that **WHOEVER BELIEVES IN HIM SHOULD NOT PERISH** but **have eternal life**. ¹⁷For God did not send his Son into the world to condemn the world, **but in order that THE WORLD MIGHT BE SAVED THROUGH HIM**. ¹⁸**WHOEVER BELIEVES IN HIM IS NOT CONDEMNED**, but **whoever does not believe is condemned already**, because he has not believed in the name of the only Son of God.   (John 3:16-18 ESV)

Electionists are committed to their doctrine of <u>*selected election*</u>[1]. It is true that our Lord died on the cross in particular for those He was to save. Our Lord did not die a generalized death as some incorrectly assume. Christ Jesus died in particular for only the redeemed. Still, the door into eternal life is **available to all**, but eternal life is given only through Jesus Christ. God in His sovereignty sets the standard. The Lord our God provided redemption for **all mankind**. Nevertheless, anyone outside the redemption of Christ Jesus shall most definitely perish in their sin forever. Each person will perish for his sins, but if anyone hears the Gospel and rejects it, his/her condemnation is even more severe.

There are many who profess faith in Christ:

Watch out my friend, *"confession of faith in Christ"* does not mean or prove that everyone actually *possesses genuine saving faith* in Christ. This is why the apostle Paul sternly warns as given by the Amplified Bible,

> Test *and* evaluate yourselves *to see* whether you are in the faith *and* living your lives as [committed] believers. Examine yourselves [not me]! Or do you not recognize this about yourselves [by an ongoing experience] that Jesus Christ is in you—unless indeed you fail the test *and* are rejected as counterfeit? (2 Cor. 13:5 AMP)

Above, the apostle is warning that just because someone acknowledges or makes an intellectual confession to the historical facts of the Gospel does not mean they are saved. Believing the historical facts of the Gospel means the person is not stupid, but knowing the facts of the Gospel does not mean a person is saved. There must be a genuine commitment and complete trust in Jesus Christ as Lord and Savior to be saved. They ought to reflect the transformation of regeneration, or else, they may still be unregenerated and sadly unsaved and lost in sin. So, there ought to be definitive evidence in the life of regeneration by the Holy Spirit.

Heaven is real, and friend listen, Hell is very real as well from which there is no turning back.

> And as it is appointed unto men once to die, but after this the judgment:
> (Heb. 9:27 KJV)

> For He says: "In an acceptable time I have heard you, And in the day of salvation I have helped you." **Behold, now *is* the accepted time; behold, now *is* the day of salvation**. (2 Cor. 6:2 NKJ)

A. Your true nature revealed

Only a fool would forsake the *saving faith in Christ*. This is because he/she is a fool: he/she missed the Gospel. They have no fear of the Lord, the living

God. (This is unfortunate but true of many associated with electronic churches across the world but unsaved.) There are others, believe or not, that attended church but only as political front. These people are without being genuinely born from above by the Spirit of God. These are people unfortunately that were never born from above by the Spirit of God, [John 3:3-7]. These people regrettably had only "*a pretense of faith*," and such people shall indeed perish forever in Hell because they did not possess genuine saving faith in Christ.

Still others concocted or manufactured "*a gospel*" and "*god*" through their carnal mind. They conceived of "*a gospel*" and "*god*" through their corrupt and depraved mind. (They have rejected in part or whole the revelation of God and refuse to submit to the standard and righteousness of God.[Rom. 10:4]) They have disregarded all the various ways God has sought to illuminate and seek to lead them to the truth.

More shockingly, many have followed the course of this world. They have turned "a deaf-ear" to the love of God. The apostle warns of the coming of the end times,

> He [*the antichrist*] will oppose and will exalt himself over everything that is called God or is worshiped, so that he sets himself up in God's temple, proclaiming himself to be God. ⁵Don't you remember that when I was with you I used to tell you these things? ⁶And now you know what is holding him back [*restraints him*], so that he may be revealed at the proper time. ⁷For the secret power [*the mystery*] of lawlessness[-*one*] is already at work; but the one who now holds it back [*restraints him*] will continue to do so till he is taken out of the way. ⁸And then the lawless one will be revealed, whom the Lord Jesus will overthrow [lit. *make an end*] with the breath of his mouth and destroy by the splendor of his coming.⁹The coming of the lawless one will be in accordance with how Satan works. He will use all sorts of **displays of power** through **signs** and **wonders** that serve **THE LIE**, ¹⁰and all the ways that wickedness **deceives those who are perishing. They perish BECAUSE they REFUSED TO LOVE THE TRUTH AND SO BE SAVED. ¹¹For this reason GOD SENDS THEM A POWERFUL DELUSION so that they will believe THE LIE** ¹²and so that **all will be condemned who have not believed** [*trusted*] **the truth but have delighted in wickedness**.   (2 Thess. 2:4-12 NIV)

Do you remember what Solomon said of those who imagine themselves righteous in their own eyes but refuse the counsel of God?

> Do you see a man who is wise in his own eyes? There is more hope for a fool than for him.   (Prov. 26:12 ESV)

As one of two doors open into eternity, the true nature of everyone will be revealed. Friend, there is no turning back from Hell once you enter its door into eternity. Remember, Jesus said,

> Enter in at the straight a gate: for it is the wide gate, and broad way that leads to destruction: and many there be which go in there at, [14]Because the gate is straight, and the way narrow that leads unto [eternal] life, and few there be that find it. [15]Beware of false prophets, which come to you, in sheep's clothing, but inwardly they are ravening wolves.
>
> (Matt. 7:13-15 GNV)

> ªNote: Only spelling is update and brackets "[ ]" are used for clarity. The phrase in v 14 is better translated by the GNV "the way narrow;" the GK word means to "compressed" or "pinched" rather than "difficult" or "hard." (See Isa. 42:1-4; Matt. 11:28-30)

Let me ask you a few questions, and be honest.

1. "Does your life demonstrate that you are genuinely born from above by the Spirit of God?"[Rom. 8:9-11]

2. "Do you know and show that you are a new creation in Christ?"[2 Cor. 5:14-17]

3. "Do you know with certainty that you have passed from death into eternal life when you believed?"[1 John 5:13]

4. "Are you definitely certain, friend, that you have passed from death into eternal life, and if so, **when** did you pass from death to eternal life?"[John 5:24] (If you do not recall when you passed from death into eternal life by faith in Christ, friend, you may still be unregenerate!)

Friend, eternal life is not a hope so or maybe. You can know with certainty that you have eternal life in Christ. God wants you to have the assurance of eternal life in Christ Jesus. The Bible is very explicit concerning knowing if you have eternal life,

> The one who believes [trusts] in the Son of God has the testimony [witness] in himself; the one who does not believe [trusting] God has made Him a liar, because he has not believed [trusted] in the testimony [witness] that God has given concerning His Son. [11]And the testimony [witness] is this, that God has given us eternal life, and this [eternal] life is in His Son. [12]He who has the Son has the [eternal] life; he who does not have the Son of God does not have the [eternal] life. [13]These things I have written to you who believe [trust]

in the name of the Son of God, SO THAT YOU MAY KNOW THAT YOU HAVE ETERNAL LIFE.   (1 John 5:10-13)

Therefore, please listen to me: the Lord wants you in Heaven. He does not desire that you perish in your sin.[1 Tim. 2:3, 4] However, you must be certain you have made a genuine commitment and you are relying and solely on Jesus' sacrifice on the cross for your sins.[2 Tim. 1:12] You need to be certain you are born from above by the Holy Spirit.[John 3:3-7; Rom. 8:3-11] When the door opens into eternity for you then your true nature will be revealed. Listen, it will be too late to change then. Make sure you genuinely possess saving faith in Christ today. Do as the apostle says, "Examine yourselves to be certain that you possess genuine saving faith of Jesus Christ the Lord."[2 Cor. 13:5] Do not trust your feeling; put your trust and confidence in God's Word.

If God were to ask you, "Why should I let you into Heaven?" What would be your answer? There is only one correct answer! Your answer must be, "Lord I have put trust in Jesus Christ who died in my place for sin and arose again on the third day."[1 Cor. 15:3, 4]

B. Unrepented and forever doom

I have saved this last section for now. This is because of the confusion and misunderstanding of presentation or sharing the Gospel with the unsaved. This is especially true, believe it or not, for those who tend to think of the Gospel on a strictly intellectual level. This is particularly referring those who endorse or hold the Gospel is reserved exclusively for the elect only. Little do they fully realize evil spirits approach the mind as though they are angels sent by God. This is a *plain biblical truth*, and it *ought to be evident* to Pastors and teachers of God's Word. Unfortunate, those steeped in tradition may try to free themselves from their "a ball and chain" but find it nearly impossible to change. I have no intention of belittling any one due to a personal higher intellectual level or the restrictive view of election. The churches need strong and formidable men and women defending and declaring the unadulterated truth of the Gospel of our Lord Jesus.

Nevertheless, some may miss or fail to grasp the simplicity and sincerity of the Gospel by viewing salvation purely and strictly on an intellectual level and divine election. **Divine election** and **will of man** are too complicated for the rational and finite mind to full comprehend. (If you think you comprehend divine election and the will of man, you are a fool!) Sincerity or coming close to the Gospel is not the same as receiving or entering into the Kingdom of God and being the recipient of redemption in Christ Jesus.

Friend, what I mean to say is that there are millions of people that confess Jesus as their Savior. Sadly however, many of these people are forever lost. They are lost because they have a **different JESUS**. They have a **counterfeit GOSPEL**. They are lost because of their false doctrine concerning Jesus Christ. If anyone has false understanding of either who Jesus is or defected understanding of the Gospel, then, they shall perish in Hell forever! Thus, they will indeed spend eternity in Hell because they failed to genuinely repent and receive the genuine **JESUS** of the Bible. Jesus Christ is the Supreme Sovereign Lord and Creator and Sustainer of all things. Still others may miss salvation because they have manufactured a religion with a futile and depraved mind, which I call *religiousology*.[2] As I have said, they also have a **different** "JESUS." They do not have the genuine Jesus presented in the Bible.

The failure to repent and receive the Gospel:

There are two extreme dangers here under this section. 1. There are people that are intellectually passive to the Gospel. 2. There are "the canned Gospel" people who have been swayed by some emotional appeal rather than illuminated and convicted power of the Holy Spirit. Friend, these are very, very serious errors. So, please, I am begging you, hear me out patiently.

1.   There are people that are intellectually passive to the Gospel.

This group strongly adheres to strict "*divine election*," but they adamantly deny the involvement of the human will. Such people among this group tend to be passive, and they wait to be divinely elected. Some among this group today have even mocked *people coming forward* or *raising their hand* to receive Christ. Still even others doubt those who pray the "*sinner's prayer*" to receive Jesus Christ. (I would be careful mocking anyone responding to the Gospel call.) Listen carefully, mocking at those that give invitations to receive Christ or mocking those responding to the Gospel, you, my friend, are in very serious danger of offering the *True One* that is wooing the unregenerate, the Holy Spirit of God!

Many among the "*divine electionists*" very rarely give a call to receive Jesus as Lord and Savior, if ever. This is especially true of those who strongly espouse the "*doctrine of divine election*" who never (**I mean never**) give an invitation to genuinely believe and receive Jesus Christ. The *divine electionists* tell people to pray, but they cannot call upon the Lord since it is by divine election. What a tragedy where tradition overrides the plain teaching of Scripture. As Jesus said,

139

> "*Thus* invalidating the word of God by your tradition which you have handed down; and you do many things such as that." (Mark 7:13)

Also, it is evident many in this group never knock on doors. They never bother to go door to door presenting the Gospel to everyone in their community. That is, they never give a clear presentation of the Gospel to others. The Gospel invitation must include the call to **confess** and **receive** Jesus Christ as Lord and Savior. *Divine electionists* cannot even give assurance of salvation. Amazingly true! The reason *divine electionists* are unable to give assurance of anyone seeking salvation is the *divine electionists* don't know if the ones seeking salvation are among the elect. How sad is that?

Below, our Lord is directing His comments to the Pharisees, but there is definite application here that equally pertains to anyone today.

> [12]For whoever exalts himself will be humbled, and whoever humbles himself will be exalted. [13]Woe to you, scribes and Pharisees, you hypocrites! You defraud widows of their houses, and for a show make lengthy prayers. Therefore you will receive greater condemnation. [14]Woe to you, scribes and Pharisees, you hypocrites! **You shut the kingdom of heaven in men's faces**. You yourselves do not enter, **nor will you let in those who wish to enter.**[b] [15]Woe to you, scribes and Pharisees, you hypocrites! You traverse land and sea to win a single convert, and when he becomes one, you make him twice as much a son of hell as you are. (Matt. 23:12-15 MSB)

> [b]Note: v 14 is omitted by many translations or place in italics because the GK text is not found in some older GK text.

Friend, your sarcasm will surely be dealt with at Judgment Seat of Jesus Christ, "the Bema Seat of Christ."[2 Cor. 5:10] (That is of course if you do not fail the test of 2 Cor. 13:5.)

There are religious groups that adamantly espouse doctrine of election without human response. Such groups adamantly adhere (as I have said above) to "*selected election*." People are left waiting passively to be one of the elect. Such churches or denominations affirm the human will **is not involved**, I suppose people wait for some *feeling* or realization that they are "*one of the elect.*"

I even heard one internationally known teacher and philosopher (and very orthodox in doctrine) raise the issue of whether or not he was among the "elect." That, my friend, is sad indeed!

The astute John Calvin and brilliant Dr. Martin Luther (even Luther was seemingly even *stronger on election* than Calvin). Listen, Calvin and Luther were outstanding men of God in their right and unequal with their tremendous godly impact on the Christian world. So, I confess that I am insignificant, very trivial, a nobody, and unfit to carry the shoes of these mighty men God. Nevertheless, I too have the Spirit of God. I too have the spirit of discernment by the Lord. But I am not without learning though I am a nobody. I certainly do not compare myself intellectually or spiritually to these mighty men of God in whom I greatly admire. We must esteem such men and their mighty contribution to Christian Community and world. These are mighty men of God that broke down what seemed as an impenetrable wall, the *infamous* Roman doctrine. These great Reformation leader and others like them freed the Gospel to the world. Even the Bible had been chained to the wall by Rome. Yet, these mighty men of God stood boldly for justification through genuine saving faith in the risen and glorified Christ Jesus.

Nevertheless, the Gospel is indeed available to everyone! Therefore, I must strongly disagree with "*selected election*!" The sovereignty of God and the will of man is an impossible paradox to fathom or comprehend by human reasoning. Humankind and even the mighty angels of God cannot unravel or comprehend the seeming enigma or conundrum of the will man and God's sovereignty.

There is good reason for humankind's inability to fully understand these two paradoxical truths. These truths seem incompatible: **sovereignty of God** and **will of humans** working in harmony. However, the Lord is not bound by time and neither is God incumbered as finite and depraved man or holy angels finite as compared to the Lord. The Lord is eternally present, and there is no past, present, or future with Him. Therefore, mankind's reasoning is locked into creation of time and so are the angels of God. Besides, mankind's reasoning flowed and totally depraved due his fall into sin and utter condemnation and alienation from God. Whereas, the Lord is *imminent* (capable of being with His creation but unaffected by time or creation). Yet, God is *transcendent* and eternally existent apart from His creation and time. Who then can understand such wonderful truths concerning the Lord our God?

Yes, the Lord knew His redeemed before the creation was unfolded, but this does not establish the doctrine of election. My friend, this is one of mysteries of the saving grace of Jesus. In the same way, the demons are allowed to hinder the Gospel upon the unbelievers,[2 Cor. 4:3, 4] but the power of the Gospel gets through to the unbelievers and people are gloriously saved.[1 Cor. 1:18, 24] Hallelujah! Humans are unable to resolves such divine mysteries.

Allow me to illustrate what I think is a <u>fallacy</u> and <u>defect</u> of "*selective election*." That is, the weakness in the teaching or belief in solely chosen by election by God without the human will.

In my upper class years in my junior or senior year in college, I had asked the professor of systemic theology this propositional question. (Keep in mind I had spent six years in the Marines, and I was in my late twenties.) I asked the professor, "If someone is elected, then, is it evident by necessity implied that the person is logically saved before he/she believes?"

Well, he *hemmed and hawed* and *hemmed and hawed* for several minutes. Then, he said, "Well, I guess you are right; you are saved before you believe." I looked at him with puzzlement and said, "But I said I have a problem with that logic. The Bible teachers that, "A person must '*believe*' to be saved." Do you know he let out one loudest *horse-laughs* I have ever heard? By the way, he was one of my dearest friends and #1 professor in my mind.

2.   The "canned Gospel" swayed by emotional appeal.

<u>Now</u> <u>to</u> the second issue: On the opposite end of the equation of <u>*selective election*</u> is solely by the "<u>human</u> <u>will</u>." As one erroneous evangelist said in his invitation with the Gospel: "The devil has voted against you, and God has voted for you. You cast the deciding vote and vote for Jesus." Such declaration is not only total bankruptcy in Biblical Theology; this is *humanism* and being *brain dead* to the plain teaching of the Scriptures.

The **devil has <u>NO</u> say**, and the **devil has <u>NO</u> vote** in anyone's eternal destiny. The **devil is finite** and **completely evil**. He shall indeed have the **lowest ebb in Hell** along with the evil angels that accompanied him.

Please pay attention: the fallacy is that solely by the <u>*will*</u> no one would be saved if it depended on strictly the will of man. Without the **wooing, illuminating**, and **convicting** power of the Holy Spirit, no one would be saved. Our Lord Jesus made this very clear.^{John 16:7-11}

The Bible is clear that **NO ONE SEEKS GOD**. Upon this, the *electionists* are indeed absolutely correct: **NO ONE SEEKS GOD**.

> As it is written, There is none righteous, no, not one: [11] There is none that *understands*, there is **none that *seeks* after God**. [12] They are all gone out of the way, they are together become unprofitable; there is none that doeth good, no, not one.   (Rom. 3:10-12 KJV)

Oh, yes, humankind does seek a ***god***; he seeks a ***god*** of his own manufacturing. That is, mankind seeks a ***god*** from his own depraved and corrupted futile mind. Humanity is total incapable of personally knowing the LORD our God (the Creator and Sustainer of all things.) Man is incapable of knowing God due his darkened alienation and wickedness of sin. The Lord alone is absolutely and infinitely holiness and righteousness. God is totally beyond comprehension of mankind and angels. So, if the Lord had not sought humanity (who is corrupt and depraved), humankind could never know the Lord. God is unknowable.

Our hearts and minds are completely corrupted by the fall of man in sin.[Rom. 5:12]

> Everyone that remains in Adam shall indeed perish in their sin. For as in Adam all die, even so in Christ shall all be made alive.
>
> (1 Cor. 15:22 KJV)

Humankind does not seek the Lord! The unregenerate mind is incapable of knowing the true God. Humanity is completely alienated from the Lord, an infinite holy and righteous God. Upon this the apostle is very clear,

> [2b]Teach them and exhort them about these things. [3]If someone spreads false teachings and does not agree with sound words (that is, those of our Lord Jesus Christ) and with the teaching that accords with godliness, [4]he is conceited and understands nothing, but has an unhealthy interest [GK *noseo, depraved mind*] in controversies and verbal disputes. This gives rise to envy, dissension, slander, evil suspicions, [5]and constant bickering by people **corrupted in their minds** and **deprived of the truth**, who suppose that godliness is a way of making a profit.
>
> (1 Tim. 6:2b-5 NET)

Where electionists go wrong is twofold: God is not willing that anyone perish.[1 Tim. 2:3, 4; 2 Peter 3:9] (It is eisegesis to limit the meaning to the elect.) Second, God indeed illuminates everyone coming into the world, and without illumination of the Holy Spirit no one would be saved.

> In him was life, and the life was the light of mankind. (John 1:4 NET)

> The true light, who gives light to everyone, was coming into the world.
>
> (John 1:9 NET)

Here is the point that is missed by those who espouse **the human will** to the exclusion of the **sovereignty of God**. *The Lord must therefore illuminate a person in order to be saved.* Furthermore, the Lord does illuminate everyone, but not everyone is illuminated on the same level in the world. Yes, some for certain have more light than others. However, everyone is responsible to respond to the light given him/her by God. If a person ignores the light from

God, then that person will perish in their sin without mercy. Regardless of man's illumination (great or small) people will perish in their sin.

Isaiah's appeal is not limited to Israel. Isaiah's appeal applies to all humanity,

> **SEEK THE LORD** while He may be found; **CALL UPON HIM WHILE HE IS NEAR**. Let the wicked forsake his way [*let them repent*] And the unrighteous man his thoughts; And let him **return to the LORD**, And **He will have compassion** on him, And to our God, For **He will abundantly pardon**. (Isa. 55:6, 7)

The apostle Paul makes this appeal,

> God that made the world, and all things that are therein, seeing that he is Lord of *heaven* and earth, *dwells* not in temples made with hands, [25]Neither is worshipped with *men's hands*, as though he needed *anything*, seeing he *gives* to all life and breath and all things, [26]And [*He*] *has* made of one blood all *mankind*, to dwell on all the face of the earth, and [*He*] *has* assigned the seasons which were *ordained* before, and the bounds of their habitation, [27]That **they *should seek* the Lord**, if so be they might *have* groped after him, and *found* him though *doubtless* he be not *far* from *every* one of *us*. [28]For in him we *live*, and *move*, and *have* our being, as also *certain* of your *own* Poets *have said*, for we are also his generation [*creation or lit. race*][b] . [29]Forasmuch then, as we are the generation [*creation, race*] of God, we ought not to *think* that ye Godhead is like *unto* gold, or *silver*, or stone *graven* by *art* and the *invention* of man.
>
> (Acts 17:24-29 GNV)

> [c]Note: no words have been changed only the spelling is updated and words in brackets ([1], [ ]) are for clarity.

> The word "generation" (GK *genos*, vv 28, 29) refers the human *race* or *nations*, but *children* or *offsprings* is a less favorable translation. I suggest *creation* of God a more favorable rendering. We are **not** *children* of God nor are we God's *offsprings*. This is the error of liberalism. Overall, the Geneva Bible remains excellent translation.

I have already declared some of the various ways God has revealed Himself. Mankind has rejected the revelations of God. Therefore, humankind has condemned himself to an eternal Hell with no recourse or appeal. The message is a simple one:

> Because if you confess with your mouth that Jesus is Lord and believe in your heart that God raised him from the dead, you will be saved.

¹⁰For with the heart one believes and thus has righteousness and with the mouth one confesses and thus has salvation. ¹¹ For the scripture says, "Everyone who believes in him will not be put to shame." ¹²For there is no distinction between the Jew and the Greek, for the same Lord is Lord of all, who richly blesses all who call on him. ¹³**For everyone who calls on the name of the Lord will be saved**.   (Rom. 10:9-13 NET)

Religiousology a _different_ "JESUS:"

Here there are very many professing to believe in Jesus Christ. The problem here is that many such people profess to believe in "Jesus," but believing in a **different Jesus**.² ᶜᵒʳ ¹¹:³, ⁴; ᴳᵃˡ.¹:⁶⁻⁹ Hence, they are preaching and teaching a **different** GOSPEL.

The Bible is clear concerning the unregenerate, the natural man. This point is often overlooked by many sincere Bible believing teachers and preachers of the Gospel.

> None of the rulers of this age understood it, for if they had, they would not have crucified the Lord of glory. ⁹However, as it is written: "What no eye has seen, what no ear has heard, and what no human mind has conceived"— the things God has prepared for those who love him— ¹⁰**these are the things God has revealed to US**ᵈ **by his Spirit. The Spirit searches all things, even the deep things of God**. ¹¹ For who knows a person's thoughts except their own spirit within them? In the same way **NO ONE KNOWS THE THOUGHTS OF GOD except the Spirit of God**. ¹²What we [ᵃˢ ᵃᵖᵒˢᵗˡᵉˢ] have received is not the spirit of the world, **but the Spirit who is from God, so that WE** [ᵃˢ ᵃᵖᵒˢᵗˡᵉˢ] **may understand what God has freely given us**. ¹³This is what WE [ᵃˢ ᵃᵖᵒˢᵗˡᵉˢ] speak, not in words taught us by human wisdom but [ᵃˢ ᵃᵖᵒˢᵗˡᵉˢ] in words taught by the Spirit, explaining spiritual realities with Spirit-taught words. ¹⁴The person [ᴳᴷ _psuchikos_, natural man, the unregenerate] without the Spirit does not accept [ᴳᴷ _dechomai_, receive: e.g., he rejects or does not welcome] the things that come from the Spirit of God but considers them foolishness, and [ᵐᵃⁿ] cannot understand them because they are discerned only through the Spirit. ¹⁵The person with the Spirit [ᵒᶠ ʳᵉᵛᵉˡᵃᵗⁱᵒⁿ] makes judgments [ᵈⁱˢᶜᵉʳⁿˢ] about all things, but such a person is not subject to merely human judgments, ¹⁶for, "Who has known the mind of the Lord so as to instruct him?" But we [ᵃˢ ᵃᵖᵒˢᵗˡᵉˢ] have the mind of Christ.   (1 Cor. 2:8-16 NIV)

145

ᵈNote: Paul is **not** discussing what is already written and revealed in Scripture. The apostle is discussing what God was revealing to the apostles right then through "divine revelation through inspiration by the Holy Spirit and exclusively in and through the apostles."

First, let me say that the carnal minded have totally disregarded the subdivision and its context. The apostle **is NOT saying** "We (every believer) have the mind of Christ."[(v 16)] Listen, the carnal Church at Corinth most certainly **DID NOT** possess the mind of Christ. Please listen even more carefully, neither do the saints today have the mind of Christ. God forbid. Perish the taught! We as saints in Christ **DID NOT** receive revelation from God today! The Bible is complete and lacking nothing. Please erase that foolish notion: "we as saints" have the mind of Christ or the idiotic notion you can receive revelation from God. The cannon of Scripture is sealed by God. However, the apostles possessed the mind of Christ.[1 Cor. 2:16]

In 1 Cor. 1-3, the apostle Paul is defending his authority as an apostle in Corinthians. Paul clarifying that all the apostles had the mind of Christ. That is, the apostles were inspired by Holy Spirit to give us the Scripture, which is unbreakable and sealed forever. This is because the apostles alone and those assisting the apostles were given the very mind of Christ by the Holy Spirit. The Holy Spirit indwelt and sovereignly worked through the chosen apostles of Christ's and those chosen and selected with them. For example, the Lord just before His ascension told the apostles,

> Then he said to them, "These are my words that I spoke to you while I was still with you, that everything written about me in the Law of Moses and the Prophets and the Psalms must be fulfilled." Then he **OPENED THEIR MINDS**ᵉ to understand the Scriptures
>
> (Luke 24:44, 45 ESV)

ᵉNote: the KJV omits the word "_minds_." Here in is the point of Paul; he and the other apostles (and those closely associated with the apostles) possessed the **mind** and **understanding** of Christ by the Spirit of God. The natural man, the carnal mind, does not receive the things of God. No one _knows_ or _understands_ the Lord apart from divine illumination and revelation, and the Lord has ceased divine revelation. Furthermore, no one able to know the true God, the Lord, based upon reason!

There are many people that unfortunately approach the Bible solely as pure and natural through carnal reasoning. They study the Bible through natural reason **AND** void of illumination by the Spirit of God. Still, the Bible is not a dead book written by the people of world. The Bible is a living book [Heb. 4:12; 1 Peter 1:23] that must be illuminated by the Spirit of the living God. This principle of the illumination by the Spirit is overlooked by some of the adamant Fundamentalists. Friend, how warped is that?

The *electionists*, of all people, should be the first to recognize the necessity of illumination by the Spirit of God. Hello! Pure reason of the natural man (unregenerate) **cannot know nor understand the Lord**. Once again, let is note Isaiah who said by the Spirit of God:

> **Seek the LORD** while He may be found; **Call upon Him** while He is near. [7]Let the wicked forsake his way [*repent*] And the unrighteous man his thoughts; And let him **return to the LORD**, And **He will have compassion** on him, And to our God, For He **will abundantly pardon**. [8]"For My thoughts are not your thoughts, Nor are your ways My ways," declares the LORD. [9]"For *as* the heavens are higher than the earth, So are My ways higher than your ways And My thoughts than your thoughts. [10]"For as the rain and the snow come down from heaven, And do not return there without watering the earth And making it bear and sprout, And furnishing seed to the sower and bread to the eater; [11]So will My word be which goes forth from My mouth; It will not return to Me empty, Without accomplishing what I desire, And without succeeding *in the matter* for which I sent it. (Isa. 55:6-11)

Today everything is so generic nowadays, "*god.*" The natural man does know the **LORD**. Yes, mankind may recognize the **LORD** as the God of the Bible, but the unregenerately, the unregenerate, the unsaved, do not know Him. To hear many in the churches, neither do they know the **LORD**. That my friend is apologizing spiritually sick!

Little do many even realize that the removal of His blessed name, **LORD**, is a judgment upon all humanity that mocked or perverted His Word in unrighteousness. The Lord has given mankind over to his ungodly and depraved mind. Paul reveals in [Romans 1:18-32] that the Lord has given mankind over to his wicked and perverted mind as a judgment upon man. The Lord has given mankind over to his depraved mind to hang himself. Let me tell you humanity has hung himself. In the same way since the churches have an insatiable craving with the world, the wickedness in the churches is ripe for judgment as well.

Conclusion

Yes, some will unfortunately misinterpret this chapter. I am sure that the Lord works all things after His own will, [Rom. 11:33-36; Eph. 1:11]. We must place our hands over our mouth and let us be astonished that anyone is saved due to wholesale corruption through the churches. For shame! As Peter says,

> And if the righteous are barely saved, what will become of the ungodly
> and sinners?   (1 Peter 4:18 NET)

Due to the Lord being an infinite holy and righteous, all humanity stands as **in bondage and a slave to sin** and **Hell bound sinners** and speechless before Him. God shall reveal the innumerable ways He has sought out rebellious and wicked humankind to save him. However, the unregenerate spurns, scorns, and rejects the grace of the Lord God.[Titus 2:11-13; Heb. 10:28-31] Like Israel, the church has hardened their hearts against the Lord.[Heb. 3:8, 15; 4:7]

Others only profess faith in Christ, but the truth of the matter is that they are completely void of any genuine commitment of faith in Christ. They only have an historical faith of the facts of the Gospel, but they are void of biblical repentance. Yes, they are void of truly trusting in the Son of God.

Still others claim faith in Christ as Lord, but these are people who trust a **different** JESUS. Yes, they are relying on a **counterfeit** GOSPEL. It is certain that the unregenerate are not looking for the **blessed hope**; they are not looking for the **mercy of the Lord unto eternal life**.[Titus 2:13; Jude 1:21]

Lastly, there are those driven by *religiousology*. Ironically, this includes the so-called atheists whose god is "mother nature," *the force*. This includes the host of religions of the world.

Perhaps I may sum up everything by what the Lord said with His tender mercy to Israel but surely His words equally apply to every human being as our blessed Lord and Savior has provided redemption for everyone,

> "Jerusalem, Jerusalem, you who kill the prophets and stone those sent
> to you, how often I have longed to gather your children together, as a
> hen gathers her chicks under her wings, and [*but*] you were not willing.
> Look, your house is left to you desolate. For I tell you, you will not see
> me again until you say, 'Blessed is he who comes in the name of the
> Lord.'"   (Matt. 23:37-39 NIV)

Footnotes:

1. *"Selected election:"* it is meant that those who teach salvation is exclusively by *divine election*. According to *divine electionists*, the human will is not involved in salvation. God in His sovereignty chose to save some people but bypass others for reasons we do not know. The result is that those that are bypassed will go to Hell. The inference

implied is that God is not giving a legitimate offer of salvation to everyone but only to the elect. Some *electionists* maintain there a general call of the Gospel, but there is no one that will respond to the Gospel. So, God chose to save some (again for reasons we do not know), and thus, God bypassed the rest of humanity, condemning them to Hell due to their sins.

2. *Religiousology*: is a coined word. *Religiousology* is any and all religions that reject, distort, or in any way seek to override the orthodox or true teaching of the OT and NT. As the apostle Peter says,

> But the word of the Lord *endures* forever. And this is the word which by the gospel is preached unto you. (1 Peter 1:25 KJV)

Part Four

Choose Eternal Life

CHAPTER 14

The Epilogue

Memory verse

"Do not marvel at this; for the hour is coming in which all who are in the graves will hear His voice and come forth-- those who have done good, to the resurrection of life, and those who have done evil, to the resurrection of condemnation." (John 5:28, 29 NKJ)

Introduction

In the memory verses, some might assume that the meaning is, "those that did good *deeds* [or *good things*] to the resurrection of life —."[v 29] The phrase "those who have done good" may be a little misleading to some people. Eternal life is God's free gift by faith in Christ.[John 5:24] Eternal life is through faith in Christ.[John 3:16] Eternal life can never be achieved by good words; there is no one good but God!

The translation is correct, but we must keep in mind that there is no one that is good but God.[Luke 18:19; Rom. 3:10-12, 23] The phrase "do good [GK *agathos*]" could just as well imply "*making the good* [*right*] *choices*." Every person must choose to receive Christ Jesus. Hence, choosing to repent and receive Christ is the "good thing to do."

Jesus said very explicitly,

> And Jesus said to him, "Why do you call Me good [*agathos*]? No one is good except God alone." (Mark 10:18)

From Luke 18:18ff (a parallel account), the man was a ruler and the man was very familiar to the Law of Moses: 'You know the commandments,' [Luke]

[18:20]. Jesus seen that he addresses Him as a mire "good Rabbi—" Our Lord said, 'Why do you call Me good [agathos]? No one is good except God alone.' David said (as we noted these verses in [Rom. 3:10-12]),

> The fool says in his heart, "There is no God." They are corrupt, doing abominable iniquity; **there is none who does good**. [2] God looks down from heaven on the children of man to see if there are any who understand, who seek after God. [3] They have all fallen away; together they have become corrupt; **there is none who does good, not even one**. (Psa. 53:1-3 ESV)

Furthermore, the Bible is clear that by the words or deeds of the Mosaic Law shall **no** person be justified or declared righteous by the works of the Law.

> Knowing that a man is not justified by the works of the law, but by the faith of Jesus Christ, even we have believed in Jesus Christ, that we might be justified by the faith of Christ, and not by the works of the law: for by the works of the law shall no flesh be justified. (Gal. 2:16 KJV)

The Law is holy and just. However, the Mosaic Law is only like a mirror: the Law reveals the holiness and righteousness of God. The Mosaic Law also reveals the sinfulness and wickedness of humankind. The Law tells the whole truth of the human heart. The Law tells the truth concerning the human nature. The Law does not impart righteousness. The Law declares what is right and what is sin. Therefore, accord to the Law, all humanity are sinners before the Lord God Almighty. So, there is no one righteous before God.

Let us be careful in understanding Jesus' words, '- those who have done good, to the resurrection of life, and those who have done evil, to the resurrection of condemnation [damnation, judgment].'[John 5:29 NKJ] There is none good, and there is certainly none that does good deeds to earn eternal life.

Friend, all that are saved, we are saved by His grace through genuine commitment of saving faith in Christ Jesus, the only Lord and Savior.

> For we also once were foolish ourselves, disobedient, deceived, enslaved to various lusts and pleasures, spending our life in malice and envy, hateful, hating one another. [4]But when the kindness of God our Savior and *His* love for mankind appeared, [5]He saved us, not on the basis of deeds which we have done in righteousness, but according to His mercy, by the washing of regeneration and renewing by the Holy Spirit, [6]whom He poured out upon us richly through Jesus Christ our Savior, [7]so that being justified by His grace we would be made heirs according to *the* hope of eternal life. (Titus 3:3-7)

The Lord our God is redeeming wicked mankind through His loving grace and mercy in Christ Jesus. The love of God (Rom. 5:8) is indeed being extended to anyone that will receive Jesus as Lord. Listen my friend, the Lord desires that you receive His love as the free gift, but His love is only offered through Jesus Christ. Otherwise, you shall surely face His infinite and furious wrath in Hell forever. Choose life in Christ today.

A. The door to Heaven is accessible to all

Friend, there is coming a day when the door to Heaven shall be shut. Yes, then, it will be too late to enter Heaven. The door will be shut. Please hear me! Yes, the Lord our God is loving, merciful, and abounding in grace. As the apostle Paul said so well as given by NAS.

> Therefore, just as through one man [Adam's] sin entered into the world, and death through sin, and so death spread to all men, because all sinned— [13]for until the Law sin was in the world, but sin is not imputed when there is no law. [14]Nevertheless death reigned from Adam until Moses, even over those who had not sinned in the likeness of the offense of Adam, who is a type of Him who was to come. [15]But **the free gift** is not like the transgression. For if by the transgression of the one [Adam's sin] the many died, much more did the grace of God and the gift by the grace of the one Man, Jesus Christ, abound to the many. [16]The gift is not like *that which came* through the one [Adam] who sinned; for on the one hand the judgment *arose* from one *transgression* resulting in condemnation, but on the other hand **the free gift** *arose* from many transgressions resulting in justification. [17]For if by the transgression of the one [Adam], death reigned through the one, much more **those who receive** the abundance of grace and of **the gift of righteousness** will reign in life through the One, Jesus Christ. [18]So then as through one [Adam's] transgression there resulted condemnation to all men, even so through one act of righteousness [of Jesus Christ] there resulted justification of life to all men. [19]For as through the one man's [Adam's] disobedience the many were made sinners, even so through the obedience of the One [Jesus Christ] the many will be made righteous. [20]The Law came in so that the transgression would increase; but where sin increased, grace abounded all the more, [21]so that, as sin reigned in death, even so grace would reign through righteousness to eternal life through Jesus Christ our Lord.

(Rom. 5:12-21)

155

Please note the emphasis of the "**FREE GIFT**" through "**GRACE**." Please note that the apostle Paul's appeal and emphasis is on **the FREE GIFT of GRACE**. The **FREE GIFT of eternal life is available to everyone**. Still, each person must personally repent and receive the **FREE GIFT** to have it.

> [16]And the **FREE GIFT** is not like the effect of the one man's sin. For the judgment following one trespass brought condemnation, but the **FREE GIFT** following many trespasses **BRINGS JUSTIFICATION**. [17]If, because of the one man's trespass, death exercised dominion through that one, much more surely will **THOSE WHO RECEIVE** the **ABUNDANCE OF GRACE** and the **FREE GIFT OF RIGHTEOUSNESS** exercise dominion in [*eternal*] **LIFE THROUGH** the one man, **JESUS CHRIST**. [18]Therefore just as one man's trespass led to condemnation for all, so one man's act of righteousness **LEADS TO JUSTIFICATION AND** [*eternal*] **LIFE FOR ALL**. [19]For just as by the one man's disobedience the many were made sinners, so by the one man's obedience **THE MANY WILL BE MADE RIGHTEOUS**.
>
> (Rom. 5:16-19 NRS)

Do you see it? Jesus Christ is able to make you righteous unto eternal life in Him. God is offering the wonderful free gift of eternal life through Jesus Christ. You cannot earn this eternal life; eternal life is a free gift by the grace of the Lord Jesus. But listen, you must repent and receive the free gift personally by faith calling upon the Lord Jesus Christ to save you from your sin.

This is the grace of God. His grace is the free gift, and His grace also teaches us how to live godly in our saving faith in Christ. If we have genuinely received Jesus Christ, then, we ought to be reading and studying God's Word and actively worshipping in church and serving Him. We ought to be also sharing our testimony with the unbelievers and the saints in Christ. God's Word gives us this assurance,

> [11]For the grace of God has appeared, bringing salvation to all men, [12]instructing us that, denying ungodliness and worldly desires, we should live sensibly, righteously, and godly in the present age, [13]looking for the blessed hope and the appearing of the glory of our great God and Savior, Jesus Christ, [14]who gave Himself for us that He might redeem us from all lawlessness, and purify for Himself a people for His own possession, zealous for good works. [15]These things speak and exhort and reprove with all authority. Let no one disregard you.
>
> (Titus 2:11-15 LSB)

The *electionists* are certainly zealous in their doctrine of *selective election*, but the *electionists* are adamantly in serious defective and found wanting. **Salvation is available for all** and not just the "*select few*." Nevertheless, the Lord cannot violate His infinite holiness and righteousness. Christ the Lord most certainly provided redemption for all humanity. Yes, God could have provided salvation for the *electionists*, but the Bible declares salvation indeed available for all of humanity.[John 1:29; 1 John 2:2]

The Bible is explicit that the Lord Jesus "**tasted death**" for all of mankind. Upon this, the Hebrews writer is abundantly clear,

> But we do see Jesus, who was made[a] lower than the angels for a little while, now crowned with glory and honor because he suffered death, so that **by the grace of God he might TASTE DEATH FOR EVERYONE**. (Heb. 2:9 NIV)

> [a]Note: the word "*made*" (GK *elattoo*) is referring to our Lord "*condescending*" becoming fully human.[Phi. 2:5-11] Our Lord was **not** "**made**" to be man; He willingly *condescended* taking on the humble state as a man. But He never forfeit or set aside His Deity in His incarnation. He remained completely God tabernacled in human flesh.[Psa. 2:7; John 1:14; 1 Tim. 3:16] God cannot diminish His eternal Deity.

However, I am sternly warning you: if you do not repent and commit your life and total trust in Jesus Christ as your personal Lord and Savior, you will surely perish in Hell. Furthermore, keep in mind that you stand condemned already.[John 3:18, 36] Hell is just the execution of the sentence already determined. God is giving you the opportunity to be delivered from the His wrath and the execution in Hell. You must choose; you must personally trust and receive Christ Jesus right now as your Lord and Savior.

> [9]He [Jesus Christ] was the true Light, which enlightens every man, coming into the world; [10]He was in the world, and the world was made [created] through Him, and the world did not know Him: [11]He came to [His] own, and [His] own did not receive Him; [12]but as many as received Him, to them He gave authority to become sons of God—to those believing in His Name, [13]who were begotten, not of blood, nor of will of flesh, nor of will of man, but of God. (John 1:9-13 LSV)

God is offering His love to you right now, but if you delay or refuse His love and the free gift of God, you shall perish in Hell forever and ever.

157

"And as Moses lifted up the serpent in the wilderness, even so must the Son of Man be lifted up, [15]"that whoever believes [trusts] [b]in Him should not perish but have eternal life. [16]For God so loved the world that He gave His only begotten Son, that whoever believes [trusts] in Him should not perish but have everlasting life. [17]For God did not send His Son into the world to condemn the world, but that the world through Him might be saved. [18]He who believes [trusts] in Him is not condemned; but he who does not believe [trust] is condemned already, because he has not believed [trusted] in the name of the only begotten Son of God."

(John 3:14-18 NKJ)

[b]Note: the word _believe_ is more than intellectually acknowledging the historical faith. The GK word "_pisteuo_" implies the sense of "_personal commitment_," "_personal reliance_," or "_personal trust_."

As the NRS right translates the apostle words,

And for this reason I suffer as I do. But I am not ashamed, for I know the one in whom I have put my trust [pisteuo], and I am sure that he is able to guard until that day what I have entrusted to him. (2 Tim. 1:12 NRS)

B. Otherwise Hell awaits all unregenerate

I must emphasize and be very clear: everyone outside the redemption in Jesus Christ's redemption is **condemned already**.[John 3:18] Furthermore, the Bible is very explicit, the wrath of God already abides or rests on unsaved right now.[John 3:36]

Nevertheless, there is good news by the apostle John, if anyone is willing to receive it,

[9]If we _receive_[c] the _witness_ of men, the _witness_ of God is greater: for this is the _witness_ of God, which he testified [witness] of his _Son_. [10]He that _believes_ [trusts] in that _Son_ of God, _has_ the _witness_ in _himself_: he that _believes_ not God, _has_ made him a _liar_, because he _believed_ [trusted] not ye record [witness], that God witnessed of that his _Son_. [11]And this is that record [witness], to wit, that God _has given unto_ us _eternal_ life, and this life is in that his Son. [12] He that _has_ that _Son_, _has_ that [eternal] life: and he that _has_ not that _Son_ of God, _has_ not [eternal][c] life. [13]These things _have_ I written _unto_ you, that _believe_ in the Name of that _Son_ of God, that ye may _know_ that ye _have eternal_ life, and that ye may _believe_ in the Name of that _Son_ of God. (1 John 5:9-13 GNV)

'Note: no words have been changed in the GNV. Only the spelling is updated, and the words in brackets "[ ]" are for clarity.

My friend, this is a promise God made to all human beings regardless of their wickedness of sin. God made this promise of eternal life before creation itself:

In hope of eternal life which God, who cannot lie, promised before time began.   (Titus 1:2 NKJ)

If you take a cavalier attitude and delay in your repentance and fail to make a genuine commitment in Jesus as Lord and as personal Redeemer, then you have consigned yourself to Hell forever. Your sentence is already determined. (All of us are sinners before God; therefore, everyone is under the wrath of God.) The execution of that sentence will surely be implemented at the Great White Throne Judgment. *Repent of your sin*, and *confess and receive* Jesus Christ as your Lord and Savior right now while there is still time. Friend, the Lord will speedily respond and save you immediately. Jesus will change your heart and mind for the better starting today. He will clean you up from inside out.

There is absolutely no reason for anyone to perish in Hell since God has made a provision of salvation for everyone that truly receives Jesus Christ. This is because Jesus has made the provision to save you right now. Yes, we deserve Hell, but in God's infinite mercy, He is willing to save you from your sins. However, you must repent and turn to the Lord Jesus to save you from your sin. Jesus shall surely save you right now from the penalty of sin. The Lord has provided redemption as the "**free gift by His grace**" as we noted in Romans five. Yes, my friend,

For the grace of God that bringeth salvation hath appeared to all men.

(Titus 2:11 KJV)

If you delay in responding to the loving grace, mercy, and free gift of God, you will indeed perish eternity in Hell. Jesus said for those that refuse to receive the free gift of God,

'Depart from me, you accursed, into the eternal fire that has been prepared for the devil and his angels!'   (Matt. 25:41 NET)

Why would anyone be so foolish to refuse the free gift of eternal life? Yet, this is exactly what Paul and Barnabas told the Jews that rejected the eternal life in Christ. (Many Jews refused to believe Jesus is the Messiah, the only Savior; so, don't be foolish.) Paul and Barnabas warned the unbelieving Jews,

Beware, therefore, that what the prophets said does not happen to you: [41]'Look, you scoffers! Be amazed and perish, for in your days I am doing a work, a work that you will never believe, even if someone tells you.'" [42]As Paul and Barnabas were going out, the people urged them to speak about these things again the next sabbath. [43]When the meeting of the synagogue broke up, many Jews and devout converts to Judaism followed Paul and Barnabas, who spoke to them and urged them to continue in the grace of God. [44]The next sabbath almost the whole city gathered to hear the word of the Lord. [45]But when the Jews saw the crowds [Gentiles present], they were filled with jealousy; and blaspheming, they contradicted what was spoken by Paul. [46]Then both Paul and Barnabas spoke out boldly, saying, "It was necessary that the word of God should be spoken first to you. Since you reject it **and judge yourselves to be unworthy of eternal life**, we are now turning to the Gentiles.

(Acts 13:40-46 NRS)

Friend, do not judge yourself unworthy of eternal life, but that is exactly what you will be doing if you fail to repent and trust in Jesus Christ.

I beg you to please listen; remember, Jesus said very definitely,

And fear not them which kill the body, but are not able to kill the soul: but rather fear him which is able to destroy [d] both soul and body in hell. (Matt. 10:28)

[d]Note: The word "destroy" (GK *apollumi*) does not mean *to erase, obliterate*, or *annihilate*. It means to make *inoperative* or *ineffective*. A person will continue forever in Hell.

Jesus describes Hell as,

And shall cast them into a furnace of fire: there shall be wailing and gnashing of teeth. (Matt. 13:42)

Even after the thousand-year reign of Christ and after unveiling the New Heavens and New Earth and the New Jerusalem, the Bible says,

"But the cowardly, unbelieving, abominable, murderers, sexually immoral, sorcerers, idolaters, and all liars shall have their part in the lake which burns with fire and brimstone, which is the second death."

(Rev. 21:8 NKJ)

Again, outside of the blessing of the New Heaven, we read,

> Outside are the dogs and the sorcerers and the immoral persons and the murderers and the idolaters, and everyone who loves and practices lying. (Rev. 22:15)

My friend, I know God's Spirit has warned you countless times. You can deny that God is warning you, but the truth is that God has warned many times. If you refuse the Lord and His free gift of eternal life by His grace, then, there is no one who can deliver you from the fires of Hell. You will perish in your sins in Hell forever and ever.

> Anyone who rejected the law of Moses died without mercy on the testimony of two or three witnesses. [29]How much more severely do you think someone deserves to be punished who has trampled the Son of God underfoot, who has treated as an unholy thing the blood of the covenant that sanctified them, and who has insulted the Spirit of grace? [30]For we know him who said, "It is mine to avenge; I will repay," and again, "The Lord will judge his people." [31]It is a dreadful thing to fall into the hands of the living God. (Heb. 10:28-31 NIV)

Conclusion

Friend, the most wonderful good news is Heaven is available for you. Yes, Heaven is available right now. Heaven is offered free to you through the redemption that is provided through Jesus Christ. Jesus is the Lord and Savior of all people. God is offering you forgiveness and reconciliation of your sin through the saving faith in Jesus Christ.

But you must come right now to Jesus Christ while the door of eternal life is open and available. The Bible declares, 'Behold, now *is* the accepted time; behold, now *is* the day of salvation.'[2 Cor. 6:2 NKJ]

The Bible warns us,

> And just as it is appointed for man to die once, and after that comes judgment. (Heb. 9:27 ESV)

Friend, here is God's promise to you and to each of your family members and anyone else that will repent and trust in Jesus Christ as Lord and Savior:

> "Believe in the Lord Jesus, and you will be saved-- you and your household." (Acts 16:31 NIV)

However, each person must personally repent and call upon the Lord to be saved. Any person that refuses to trust in Jesus as Lord and Savior shall indeed perish in their sin in Hell. Therefore, call upon the Lord Jesus. Here is how to call upon the Lord to be saved right now.

> Because if you **confess with your mouth that Jesus is Lord** and **believe in your heart** that God raised him from the dead, **you will be saved.** [10]For **with the heart one believes** and thus has righteousness and **with the mouth one confesses** and thus has salvation. [11]For the scripture says, "Everyone who believes in him will not be put to shame." [12]For there is no distinction between the Jew and the Greek, for the same Lord is Lord of all, **who richly blesses all who call on him**. [13]**For everyone who calls on the name of the Lord will be saved.**
>
> (Rom. 10:9-13 NET)

Friend, by refusing to call upon the Lord Jesus to save you, you are consigning yourself to an eternal Hell. God does not desire that anyone perish in their sin. The Lord would rather that you repent of your sin and call upon Jesus to save right now. The apostle Peter said,

> The Lord of that promise is not slack (as some men count *slackness*) but is *patient* toward *us*, and would *have* no man to perish, but **would all men to come to repentance**.　　　　(2 Peter 3:9 GNV)

The Holy Spirit declares through the apostle Paul,

> First of all, then, I urge that entreaties *and* prayers, petitions *and* thanksgivings, be made on **BEHALF OF ALL MEN**, [2]for kings and all who are in authority, so that we may lead a tranquil and quiet life in all godliness and dignity. [3]This is good and acceptable in the sight of God our Savior, [4]**WHO DESIRES ALL MEN TO BE SAVED** and **TO COME TO THE KNOWLEDGE OF THE TRUTH**. [5]For there is one God, *and* one mediator also between God and men, *the* man Christ Jesus, [6]**WHO GAVE HIMSELF AS A RANSOM FOR ALL**, the testimony *given* at the proper time.　　　　(1 Tim. 2:1-6)

Don't say to yourself, "I will take my chances." The Bible is very clear that anyone that does not receive Jesus as Lord is condemned already.[John 3:18, 36] Do not let pride hinder you from making the decision for eternal life in Christ.

Do not believe the *electionists and their* error that God has only a *selected* a few to be saved. Repent and believe and receive Jesus Christ right now. This is the promise that comes from God who cannot lie.

> In hope of eternal life which God, who cannot lie, promised before time began.　　　　(Titus 1:2 NKJ)

Because God wanted to make the unchanging nature of his purpose very clear to the heirs of what was **promised**, he confirmed it with **an oath**. [18]God did this so that, by two unchangeable things[e] in which **it is impossible for God to lie**, we who have fled to take hold of the hope set before us may be greatly encouraged. [19]We have this hope as an **anchor for the soul, firm** and **secure**. It enters the inner sanctuary behind the curtain [*the holy of holies*], [20]where our forerunner, Jesus, has entered on our behalf. He has become a high priest forever, in the order of Melchizedek.   (Heb. 6:17-20 NIV)

[e]Note: God sealed eternal life in Christ "**with the promise** and **swearing with an oath**."

Believe on the Lord Christ and you shall be saved!

ABBREVIATIONS AND ACRONYMS

ABPE = Aramaic Bible in Plain English
AFV = A Faithful Version
AKJV = American King James Version 1999, by Michael Peter (Stone) Engelbrite
AMP = Amplified Bible
ARA or ARC = Aramaic
ASV = American Standard Version
BSB = Berean Study Bible and BLB = Berean Literal Bible
BYZ = Byzantine manuscripts
CEB = Common English Bible
CEV = Contemporary English Version
cf. = clarified
Coptic = referring Egyptian text; Egyptian Christians
Coverdale Bible = Miles Coverdale Bible 1535
CSB or HCSB = Holman Christian Standard Bible
1 Chro. = 1 Chronicles, OT
2 Chro. = 2 Chronicles, OT
1 Cor. = 1 Corinthians, NT epistle
2 Cor. = 2 Corinthians, NT epistle
CJB = Complete Jewish Bible
DBT = Darby Bible Translation,
Deut. = Deuteronomy, OT
Ecc. or Eccl. = Ecclesiastes, OT
ENG = English
Eph. = Ephesians, NT epistle
ERV = English Revised Version, 1885
ESV = English Standard Version
Ezek. = Ezekiel, OT
f = the following verse
ff = the following verses
Gal. = Galatians, NT epistle
Gen. = Genesis, OT
GK = Greek NT

GNV = Geneva Bible (1599 edition) Bible Gateway

GNT = Good News Translation

GWT = God's Word Translation

HEB = Hebrew language of the OT

Heb. =Hebrews, NT epistle

Isa. = Isaiah, OT

ISV = International Standard Version

James = NT epistle

Job = book of the OT

John = the Gospel of John, NT

1 John = the First Epistle of John, NT epistle

2 John = the Second Epistle of John, NT epistle

3 John = the Third Epistle of John, NT epistle

Josh. = Joshua, OT

Jude = NT epistle

Judges = book of the OT

1 Kings = book of the OT

2 Kings = book of the OT

KJV = King James Version; NKJV = New King James Version

lit. = literally

Latin = LAT.

Latin/English = LAT/ENG

LSV = Literal Standard Version 2020

Luke = the Gospel of Luke, NT

LVE = Latin Vulgate in ENG

LXE (& LXA) = GK OT (Septuagint) in ENG

LXX = Septuagint, GK OT

Mark = Gospel of Mark, NT

MSS = manuscript(s)

Matt. or Mat = Gospel of Matthew

MSG = The Message

NAS = New American Standard2020 and Update 1995

NCV = New Century Version

NEB = New English Bible

NEH = Nehemiah, OT

NHEB = New Heart English Bible, update 201 e

NIV = New International Version
NKJV = New King James Version, Thomas Nelson, 1982
NLT = New Living Translation
NRS = New Revised Standard 1989
NT = New Testament
OT = Old Testament
p = page
pp = pages
OJB = Orthodox Jewish Bible
1 Peter = NT epistle
2 Peter = NT epistle
Psa. = Psalm, OT
Phi. Or Phil. = Philippines, NT epistle
PTL = Praise the Lord
PNT or Philips NT = J B Philip's NT
Prov. = Proverbs, OT
Rev. = Revelation, NT epistle
Rom. = Romans, NT epistle
1 Tim. = 1 Timothy, NT epistle
2 Tim. = 2 Timothy, NT epistle
1 Sam. = 1 Samuel, OT
1 Thess. = 1 Thessalonians, NT epistle
2 Thess. = 2 Thessalonians, NT epistle
TNT = Tyndale New Testament, 1534
Titus = NT epistle
TRE = Textus Receptus in ENG (GK text of the KJV)
VUL = Latin Vulgate
WBT = Webster's Bible Translation
WEB = World English Bible
WNT = Weymouth NT
WYC = Wycliffe Bible
YLT = Young's Literal Translation

Books, tracts, and songs by the author

Books by the author
Understanding Salvation by Faith in Christ
Understanding the Biblical Principles of Bible Study
Understanding the Biblical Principles of Witnessing
Understanding Prayer
Understanding Christian Doctrine, vol. 1: The Doctrine of God
Understanding Christian Doctrine, vol. 2: The Doctrine of Creation
Understanding Christian Doctrine, vol. 3: The Doctrine of Redemption
A Short Outline on Christian Doctrine
Christ's Supreme Sovereignty Over All (Commentary on Hebrews)
The Seven Mandates of Christ
Two of the Greatest Truths in Universe and their Significances
The Greatest Contemplation of Thought Ever!
Christ the Lord, the absolute center of Theology
Meeting the Greatest Friend You'll Ever Have
The Way of the Lord more Accurately
The Lord is Faithful who calls you into His Kingdom (A Study in 1 Thessalonians)
Earnestly Contend for the Faith, (Study of the Epistle of Jude)
Two Doors into Eternity

Gospel Tracts
Eternal Life, Yours for the Asking
Have You Received the Gift of God?

Songs
Thou Art Worthy, O Lamb of God (Chair song set to music)
Tis All to Him I Owe (not set to music)
Jesus' Precious Blood Avails for You (not set to music)
Mangrove Song (Filipino children's song in English, to the tune: I'm in the Lord's Army)

Index